FROM PHYSICAL PLACE TO VIRTUAL SPACE

HOW TO DESIGN AND HOST TRANSFORMATIVE SPACES ONLINE

GWEN STIRLING-WILKIE

BMI Publishing
Bushe-Marshak Institute for Dialogic Organization Development
3898 Trenton Place
North Vancouver, BC
Canada V7R 3G5
www.b-m-institute.com

Library and Archives Canada Cataloguing in Publication
Title: From physical place to virtual space : how to design and host transformative spaces online / Gwen Stirling-Wilkie.
Names: Stirling-Wilkie, Gwen, author.
Description: Series statement: BMI series in dialogic organizational development ; 5 | Includes bibliographical references.
Identifiers: Canadiana 20210130024 | ISBN 9781777184629 (softcover)
Subjects: LCSH: Organizational change. | LCSH: Leadership. | LCSH: Virtual reality in management. | LCSH: Virtual work teams.
Classification: LCC HD58.8 .S75 2021 | DDC 658.4/06—dc23

ISBN: 978-1-7771846-2-9
Imprint: BMI Publishing

Page design: Vancouver Desktop Publishing Centre

Contents

Foreword by the Series Editors

The term Dialogic Organization Development was first used in a 2009 article we published in The Journal of Applied Behavioral Science. In that article, we wanted to describe how we had seen organization development evolve and contrast it with the original form of OD, which we labeled Diagnostic OD. We were unhappy with how OD textbooks continued to treat the newer premises and practices as if they fit the earlier model. We wanted to create a space for people to think about, research, develop, and discuss these newer approaches to change. This book series is a continuation of that ambition and purpose.

Dialogic OD is a still developing mindset (rather than a set of specific methods). It is rooted in two key intellectual movements that are influencing all social science: how social reality is constructed, maintained, and changed by how we talk (post-modernism), and how social systems emerge and self-organize without leadership direction or a plan (complexity science). We have written several articles and book chapters about this, and readers of this book (and all books in the series) are encouraged to access our website, www. B-M-Institute.com, Most of our writings and those of some others are available there for free. The articles and book chapters at the website provide a general overview of the theory of Dialogic OD, how it is the same and different from Diagnostic OD, and the basic ideas about leadership, consulting, change and creating great organizations embedded in Dialogic OD.

Since 2005 we have devoted much of our time and attention to conceptualizing and explaining Dialogic OD. Now we are turning our attention to encouraging presentations of specific dialogic practices applicable to all change methods and approaches. Each of the books in this series is a short, focused, and most important, practical exploration of one topic intended to continue expanding the theory and practice of Dialogic OD. We hope you enjoy the books. We welcome proposals for further volumes.

If you are relatively new to this set of ideas, you can download and read the free "Companion Booklet to the BMI Series in OD" by visiting www.b-m-institute.com website.

July 2019
Gervase R. Bushe
Robert J. Marshak

Author Acknowledgements

Writing this book while working on a significant consulting project has been rewarding and frustrating in equal measure. There were times when I really wanted to stop and capture what I was experiencing and learning but didn't have the time or headspace. Conversely, there were times when the last thing I wanted to do was write and successfully found many ways to distract myself.

I'd like to express my gratitude to several people, as without them this book would not have been possible.

Gervase Bushe and Bob Marshak for their invitation to expand my early writing on virtual facilitation into a book for this Dialogic OD Series. This is the first book I've written and I'm grateful for Gervase's patience, guidance and support throughout this process.

Neil Wilkie, my husband and soulmate, for taking care of everything while I was deep into writing; for his wholehearted encouragement and love, and for his unwavering belief in me when I doubted myself.

Andrea Adams, Bridget Jolliffe and Ali Herdman for their support, encouragement and many conversations during our time working together in 2020 when we all had to adapt our consulting approaches due to the pandemic. Those experiences helped develop and refine my thinking and provided me with a safe space to experiment and learn.

Joan Scarrott for her support, encouragement and contributions to developing my thinking on the psychological impact of working online.

Rob Geraghty (Presenting Virtually) for his generosity during the pandemic, creating and sharing videos on making impactful virtual presentations

The NTL Alumni Community for all of the WhatsApp group conversations where we shared and explored our learning in this arena, particularly Katherine Handy-Woods, who generously shared her expertise with me and others in the community in the early stages.

The OD Network Europe conference team led by David Nicholson for the virtual events and conferences they offered where I could explore and learn.

My final thanks go to my consulting colleagues and the client teams I worked with during 2020. They provided me with a great opportunity to apply my dialogic OD skills in a new way, develop my thinking, and experiment with new approaches. — Gwen Stirling-Wilkie, January 2021

Introduction

This book was written in the context of an unexpected global COVID-19 pandemic and subsequent disruption that fundamentally changed the way we all work. The way that we create and reinvent the spaces and 'containers' for our work as Dialogic Organization Development (OD) consultants is shifting too.

At the start of the COVID-19 pandemic in March 2020, many consultants and consulting companies found themselves poorly-equipped to work in virtual spaces. Many people (myself included) thought that bringing groups together to host and facilitate transformative change entirely in a virtual space could not be achieved in an effective, productive way. Yet the disruption of our current practices has been so significant that we have been forced to adapt and work in ways we have never considered before. We are called on to think creatively about how we use technology as an enabler to co-create or generate, as well as to transmit and share information. *The disruptors have themselves been disrupted.*

Within this new space lie generative opportunities for creating different ways to support organizations and society through the phases of reconfiguration and regeneration that are still emerging.

In our shift from the 'physical place', where our work was formerly carried out, to the current 'virtual space' where we find ourselves residing, we need to be thoughtful about the spaces or 'containers' we create for our work when they are not in the physical realm. The design of an intervention delivered in a single container, or a series of sequenced interventions in multiple containers, needs to be considered differently so that people are primed and ready for full participation.

This new way of working has forced me to look at my practice, how I design, host and facilitate. I believe we are being asked to bring some of our deeply-held design principles into the light and look at them with new eyes.

There are three questions that I've been holding and exploring over the last few months that I attempt to answer in this book:

1. **What does great design look like in virtual spaces?**

2. **How do you create sufficient connection and safety so that people feel able to contribute fully in a virtual space?**

3. **How do you increase levels of intensity and use relational dynamics to create transformative moments that matter?**

Who is this book for?

This book is for consultants and leaders who work with or are open to the Dialogic mindset approach to change and transformation in organizations. This approach involves as many of the people who are impacted by the changes as possible, and where there are no immediate 'right' answers provided by experts or an elite few. (Bushe & Marshak, 2015)

You may or may not be familiar with the term Dialogic Organization Development, or taking a social sciences approach to change and transformation. Still, you are curious to learn how to adapt some of the approaches you've used before into a virtual space. If Dialogic OD is new to you, I strongly encourage you to start by reading the Companion booklet available by registering for free at www.b-m-institute.com

You want to know how to get the best from the many available online platforms to bring about the transformation you are leading or supporting, whether as a leader or OD professional working inside an organization, or as an external OD consultant helping to shape and deliver transformation with your clients.

This book isn't about running online meetings, training courses, or leadership development programs, but many of the tips and approaches I share will also help you do that well.

You can read the whole book through from cover to cover. Alternatively, there are two parts to the book and each chapter is written as a standalone, so you can dive into a section that draws you in from the title. However you choose to read it, I hope you enjoy what follows.

A bit about me

I've been working as an independent organization development (OD) and transformation consultant for 20 years. I've worked in several different industries and sectors for a wide range of clients in the UK, Europe, and further afield. My clients range from the National Health Service and associated health care providers in the UK to multinational and global companies operating in technology, distribution, media, pharmaceutical, transport, and energy. This diverse client base enables me to have a richness of knowledge and experience to draw upon.

I describe my working style as: relational, participatory, and systemic, and my work tends to be focused on the following areas:

- Shaping and supporting organizational transformation and culture change initiatives

- Building transformation and strategic leadership capability in senior leaders and internal transformation leads

- Executive/senior team development

- High potential leader development programs

One thing I have always loved about the work I do is the process of design, whether it is creating a standalone intervention or series of interventions to deliver a specific purpose. These interventions are given a myriad of names: a workshop, a focus group, a conference, a conversation space, an event, a summit, or a system gathering. In Dialogic OD we refer to these as containers. All have a similar intent—to bring a large or small group of people together to explore, generate, align, and act, often in the name of transformation, transforming outcomes for patients or transforming how a business is structured and operates to deliver its products or services.

A summary of what's to come

This book provides practical and instructional ideas and tools to design, host and facilitate transformative spaces online. I share ways that I and others have discovered to create different and powerful intervention containers; containers that retain the essence of the relational dynamics that underpin our work and that are delivered in virtual spaces.

I will describe this through my experiences working with colleagues and clients during 2020, particularly my role in shaping and leading a critical project within a wider transformation program. **The project that I led was delivered entirely in virtual spaces. I never physically met my client, nor any of the 600+ people from five different businesses involved in this highly participative and co-creative project.**

I intend to equip you to consult with confidence as you do your work in virtual spaces. I also want to provoke our thinking as OD practitioners on the difference between taking a physical place-based intervention and making it work in a virtual space, and intentionally creating something designed for a virtual space. I believe we will need to effectively consult and work in virtual spaces long past the end of the current pandemic.

Online platforms for virtual working

As I write this, there are three leading online platforms that best support online workshops, meetings, or events through video conferencing software. Each has different features that support the kind of work we do—real-time chat/instant messaging, screen sharing, working in smaller groups, and call recording. These platforms are being constantly updated and refined. Newer platforms are available with some or all of these features, and more are being launched every month.

- Zoom
- Microsoft Teams (MS Teams)
- Google Meet (G Meet)

My platform of choice is Zoom. Of the current options available, I believe it gives the greatest flexibility and range of features for my Dialogic OD consultancy work. I know some organizations have restrictions on the platforms available to them, which may impact the choices you have when designing and hosting virtual workshops.

In some sections of the book, I refer to different features available on Zoom. These, or something similar, exist on other platforms but may be named or configured differently.

What are transformative moments?

There's an important distinction between 'transformative' and 'transformational'.

Hosting and facilitating a transformative space creates possibilities, the kind of possibilities that could ignite a spark or be a catalyst that triggers transformation. It is a generative space, which means it focuses on creating new ideas, opportunities and the motivation to act on them. On the other hand, transformational relates to a significant change that is more planned and structured, which leads to transformation.

'Transformative' describes the spaces that I create and host as a Dialogic OD consultant. My dialogic practice's key focus is bringing together mid-sized working groups, executive teams, and other key stakeholders for meaning-making and generative conversations that develop a strategy or create a shift in culture and performance.

Because of the emergent nature of things created through engaging diverse groups in inquiry and generative conversations, I never really know what will be created during a working session or series of conversations. There is a kind of hopefulness, an unexpressed potential I find exciting.

I don't go in as a content expert on the topic, already knowing the answer that should come out of the other side, or as a sector expert who knows the business environment and brings in 'best practice' from others. I go in as a curious guide and host. As Dialogic OD Professionals, our expertise is in creating generative conversations that enable or unlock the transformative potential. I explore what it takes to produce transformative moments in more depth in Chapter Seven.

A transformative space has the power to transform individual leaders so that they, in turn, can transform the interactions they have with others—what they choose to talk about and the way they choose to have that interaction. They will impact, and in turn be impacted by, that exchange and continue to transform others in future cycles of conversations held in similar ways. In this way, transformation occurs one conversation at a time (Shaw, 2002).

Designing for transformative moments is about sequencing activities to provide an arc or framework for moving a group of people into different cognitive and relational spaces, new ways of interacting, and thinking together. From initial design concepts into conversations with clients and design teams, onto paper and an agenda, then finally into the room, into that physical place (a workshop room, conference room, meeting room, or outdoor space, as it used to be before the 2020 pandemic struck).

Our role is as a creator of containers, the convener of spaces and places where participants collaborate to do the necessary work to move something forward to the next stage. We work from a dialogic mindset in the space where there are often no fixed outcomes or no single 'right' outcome, where things emerge in a socially-constructed way in the conversations and interactions between those present.

Hosting generative conversations requires a design and foundational session plan, which only provides a starting point. We know and trust that it will change once things start to happen in the room (McKergow, 2020). Our work is 'live', responding to what we see unfolding, being aware of what is happening in the group, reading others in that moment, and adjusting.

Transformative Spaces Online©

The Transformative Spaces Online framework (TSO) was developed during the process of writing this book—reflecting on my experiences and those of others. *Figure 1* below shows the framework with the key elements required to design and host transformative spaces online.

The first—**Preparing The Virtual Space**—covers the four key elements needed to prepare the virtual space for you and your clients to step into.

The second—**Mastering Virtual Consulting**—covers key relational dimensions needed to master virtual dialogic consulting, and also the future of virtual OD.

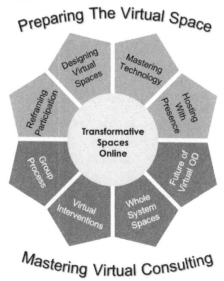

Figure 1: The Transformative Spaces Online framework

An overview of each chapter

The TSO framework provides a visual guide for the book:

Chapter One: Introduction

In this chapter, I summarize the pandemic's impact on our work as Dialogic OD consultants as we pivot from working in physical places to working in virtual spaces. I share my description of transformative moments and hypothesize that it is possible to create transformative moments that matter through the way we approach the design and hosting of the generative containers we create online.

PART 1: PREPARING THE VIRTUAL SPACE

Chapters Two-Five outline the key design concepts that create containers for Dialogic OD, with an additional focus on mastering the key technology features that generate high levels of engagement and interaction from participants.

Chapter Two: Reframing Participation

This chapter focuses the reader on the containers featured in this book: workshops and large group events. The chapter introduces two key concepts that are foundation blocks for virtual Dialogic OD and which reframe the concept of participation: widening the *Frame of Participation* and how to prepare workshop attendees for *Active Participation*. The chapter concludes with a basic workshop design for a virtual space

Chapter Three: Designing Virtual Spaces

In this chapter, I share design principles that inform the shape and nature of a program arc—the 'birds' eye' overview of a sequence of different containers created for a program of work in the virtual world. The reader is introduced to another key concept of four distinct design options that can be combined in multiple ways to create a tailored program arc for a client.

Chapter Four: Mastering Technology

This chapter explores key features available on virtual platforms and the best ways to incorporate them into virtual designs to generate high levels of participant engagement and interaction. I suggest ways to build participation and interaction synchronously and asynchronously, and explore some of what we lose through virtual interactions.

Chapter Five: Hosting With Presence

This chapter explores aspects of how we use our presence as a host to support the group or team's work online. I share some of the critical differences that impact our online presence and how we can create psychological safety online.

PART 2: MASTERING VIRTUAL CONSULTING

Chapters Six-Nine discuss how to adapt relational dimensions and common Dialogic OD methods to virtual consulting

Chapter Six: Group Process

In this chapter I look at the first two elements of group process: noticing and tracking, and how we can adapt this Dialogic OD practice to working in a virtual space.

Chapter Seven: Making Virtual Interventions

This chapter looks at the third element of group process, sharing different ways to intervene during virtual workshops to improve the group's functioning. The final section of the chapter shares how our personal presence combines with the group's process to create transformative moments that matter.

Chapter Eight: Whole System Spaces

In this chapter, I look at how to adapt some of the common dialogic large group approaches for virtual spaces. These approaches, where representatives of the whole system come together, have traditionally been run over a single day or several consecutive days.

Chapter Nine: A Virtual Dialogic OD Assignment

This chapter is a look behind the scenes on a client project where all of the ideas introduced in the book are put into action over eight months. I describe how I built a relationship with a brand-new client that I never met, the different design choice points I made, and what informed those choices. In the final pages of the chapter I reflect on what emerged that was unexpected and consider what I would have done differently.

Conclusion: Future of Virtual Dialogic OD

The final chapter looks at how two different aspects of technology are evolving and shifting how we work. The book concludes with the thought that, despite the ever-evolving advances in technology we will need to embrace, our ongoing success as Dialogic OD practitioners relies more on the choices we make; choices of how to best sequence and configure the design of virtual spaces, along with our ability to bring the best of our presence and skills in human systems in service of the client systems we work in and support.

The real-life examples we'll explore in this book

In the book I'll share examples from working in a virtual space with clients—work that started in March 2020, just as COVID-19 appeared on the scene.

My clients are five specialist businesses operating within a Group structure. They weren't used to working on virtual platforms as their operating environment is quite traditional with everything happening across several production sites and run as separate businesses. They took the decision to continue with a planned transformation program despite the impact of COVID-19 on their operations.

This assignment required me to deliver everything through a virtual platform. Had somebody said to me a month prior that I would be doing Dialogic OD without physically being in a room with everybody, I would have said "That's ridiculous! It can't be done." But I've had my preconceptions challenged and been surprised and delighted with what has emerged, and I've relished the challenge of discovering what is possible.

PART ONE

Preparing the Virtual Space

TWO

Reframing Participation

This chapter starts by comparing a range of five virtual containers and what they are best used for, before identifying the two containers that will form the focus of this book—Workshops and Large Group Events.

Two key concepts that are foundation blocks for virtual Dialogic OD are introduced. These reframe the concept of participation that is so critical to successful virtual consulting: widening the *Frame of Participation*, and how to prepare workshop attendees for *Active Participation*. The chapter concludes with a basic workshop design for a virtual space

Virtual Containers

Many virtual containers can be used effectively for different kinds of work. Here are outlines of the five most common and how they can best be utilized as virtual spaces. This book focuses on two: **Workshops and Large Group Events.**

Workshops

A well-designed online workshop can become the core container for creating transformative spaces during a transformation program. Workshops are frequently the main approach to get work done through intact teams, working groups, project teams, and stakeholder groups.

In a virtual space, workshops can promote collective meaning-making, generate ideas and solutions, build trust and relationships, establish or strengthen a 'team' culture, and align groups for action. They can range in size from a small group of five or six to a larger group of up to 30. Depending on the purpose and content, when participants' numbers grow above 30, a different container may be more appropriate—either a large group event for participative working, or a webinar for transmission of information and less interaction.

Selecting the most appropriate workshop size, methodology, and process is vital in a virtual space as it is in a physical place. The design of online workshops needs to consider the purpose and outcomes needed and the appropriate technology tools to deliver that. They are most effective online when they incorporate an element of working in small groups using breakout rooms.

Large Group Events

Bringing large numbers of people together into a transformative space from within a single system or across multiple systems can fulfil many purposes and outcomes in a dialogic approach to transformation. These large gatherings have become common in the physical place to surface and explore common issues or systemic challenges and generate new narratives, solutions, and align groups for action. They often use one or more Dialogic OD large-group methodologies like Open Space, World Café, and Appreciative Inquiry.

Transferring these into a virtual space can be tricky, and they require care and thoughtful design. It is possible to run Open Space and World Café style elements within virtual group events that give participants the freedom to follow their curiosity and energy as the event unfolds and topics emerge.

Technical production and other specialist support are essential to take care of the many technical considerations and multiple breakout spaces needed to work with large numbers of participants. These kinds of events are typically run for groups of 30+.

Below are three other common containers that have moved to virtual spaces that we will not cover in this book:

Meetings

The container of a meeting provides the key drumbeat of an organization and the delivery of purpose, intent, and outcomes. Meetings are held over a range of durations and frequencies: daily check-in and priority meetings, weekly team meetings, and monthly business review meetings, to name a few. The format of these has been shifting to online platforms for many years, and this has been accelerated during 2020, along with the need for thoughtful agenda design and chairing.

While project team meetings form part of a transformation program, these aren't explicitly covered in this book. Many of the hints and tips shared can here be applied to meeting agenda design and chairing.

Webinars

A webinar is a presentational event that is delivered online. In a webinar, one or more speakers deliver presentations or instructional material to attendees in transmit mode. These have limited interactivity; often just questions submitted centrally or through Chat. Webinars can be delivered live or pre-recorded for transmission at a set time, and the link for a recorded webinar can be shared to be watched on-demand.

Webinars can be effectively used when needing to communicate the same information in a consistent manner to many people. Group size can be as large as required; webinars are commonly attended by hundreds, or even thousands, of people at once.

Online courses, programs, and virtual training sessions

These are designed to build specific knowledge or skills and are delivered either as a one-off training session or as a course with a sequence of structured and planned modules. These are similar to workshops, as they are designed with high interactivity and participation (Bushe has recently coined the term '*webaworkshop*', to distinguish these from webinars). But the purpose is different from workshops that are part of a Dialogic OD program. The sequencing and design of a program or course is very different from one which happens face to face. A two-day training course previously delivered in person would need careful redesigning to be delivered successfully online over a number of sessions.

These can be created for teams to access together (synchronous or live) or pre-recorded to access on-demand if designed in that way (asynchronous). A course can combine elements of both.

There may be elements of a transformation program that require the development of new skills and knowledge in large groups of people. A single session or modular course could provide this, supplemented by virtual application groups to encourage new skills to be embedded.

These can be delivered to large numbers of people at the same time, in multiple locations.

Reframing Participation

One of the key considerations when running workshops and events in a virtual space is the need to reframe the concept of 'participation'. In a physical place, the time window of the workshop itself is the main point of participation (e.g. a full-day or half-day workshop).

In virtual spaces, we need to embrace a wider time frame for participation, one that extends beyond the time boundary of the workshop itself. This is one of the most critical aspects of creating transformative spaces online.

In a physical place workshop, we typically send out information a week or so beforehand regarding the purpose and intended outcomes for the workshop, together with an agenda. At the workshop itself, we allow time for input sessions where the context and background to the workshop is shared at the start of the day to explain things in more detail, or where a critical concept or framework might be introduced before inviting exploration and contribution by participants.

Figure 2 shows the 'Frame of Participation' in a physical place workshop in the center block, preceded by the agenda, and concluded by some follow-up activity.

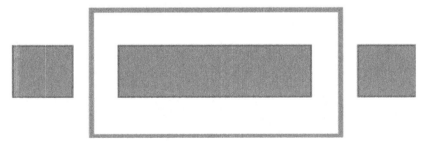

Figure 2: Physical Place Frame of Participation

In virtual spaces, people get tired faster, so workshops need to be shorter and more focused. Our concentration spans are less, and we soon become exhausted as we use up more energy working online. This appears to be caused by our inability to pick up on the kinds of social cues we are used to. It takes more energy for our brains to process what we are experiencing, hence our exhaustion *(health.com, 2020)*. As a result, people have a lower tolerance and are easily distracted. The phenomenon of 'Zoom fatigue' or being 'Zoomed out' is heard when people move from one online meeting or workshop to the next without a sufficient gap, or attend long meetings or workshop sessions online without breaks.

The impact of this on designing workshops for virtual spaces is that the time spent online needs to be geared towards active participation to maximize everyone's contribution. This means less time on input and background during the actual workshop and requires a different way to prepare people, so they arrive ready for active participation.

Figure 3 shows the wider Frame of Participation that is needed for a virtual workshop. There are two active phases within the Frame of Participation: the first is a preparation phase, and the second is the workshop itself. These are preceded by the invitation and concluded by some follow-up activity.

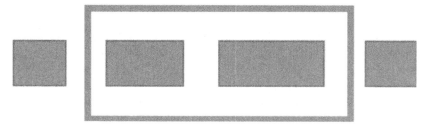

Figure 3 Virtual Space Frame of Participation

The Frame of Participation

Let's take a deeper look into what is included in the Frame of Participation. It is divided into four stages which span from inviting someone to attend a workshop through to follow-up action afterwards. *Tables 1 and 2* contrast the difference between a face-to-face workshop and the extended Frame of Participation for a virtual workshop. There is more preparation required to enable active participation in the shorter online session.

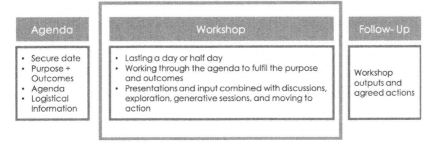

Table 1: Physical Place Detailed Frame of Participation

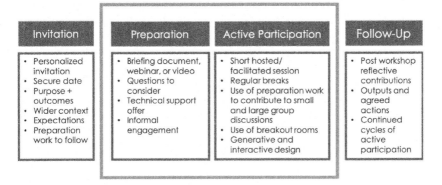

Table 2: Virtual Space Detailed Frame of Participation

Design Considerations

The Frame of Participation can be used to plan and shape the timing and design for each of your virtual containers' four stages: Invitation, Preparation, Active Participation, Follow-Up Action.

Map what needs to be considered and included in each of the four stages to deliver the purpose/outcomes for the workshop as a standalone event or as part of a sequence of interventions:

1. **Invitation:** Secure the date in participants' calendars, share context and background for the workshop, and indicate preparation work that needs to be completed.

2. **Preparation:** Send out the information that needs to be shared ahead of the workshop and any briefing or preparation activity that needs to occur, so participants arrive ready for Active Participation.

3. **Active Participation:** The design of the online workshop itself, the methodology and approaches to achieve the outcomes, the use of breakout rooms, the method to capture outputs etc. These are explored in more detail in Chapter 4.

4. **Follow-Up:** This may contain outputs from the workshop, an opportunity to continue contributing, confirm actions that were agreed upon, and identify any specific accountable items.

Preparing people for Active Participation

The Invitation and Preparation stages in *Table 2* are the first two elements that help to prepare people for active participation at the workshop. The third is the design and hosting of the workshop itself.

Invitation

This is essentially the same whether the work is being done in a physical or virtual setting; consider who the invitation should be sent from, include the date and time of the workshop, the purpose and intended outcomes, where this particular workshop fits within the broader view of the transformation program (if that is relevant), why this person is being invited, and your expectations of them (what you believe their unique contribution will be). Set expectations for the timing and amount of the preparation work to follow. The nature of good invitations is covered in more detail in McKergow (2020), and you should be familiar with the opportunities a 'generative image' provides for constructing powerful invitations (Bushe, 2020)

Preparation

The Preparation phase should ensure that participants turn up ready to engage with a good level of contextual understanding. They will have completed any activity or individual meaning-making, enabling them to contribute to the workshop's intended purpose more quickly than they would at a face-to-face workshop.

To decide what needs to be included in the preparation information, consider these questions:

1. What do you need people to read or see before they join the session?

2. What questions do you want them to consider beforehand for them to do some individual meaning-making?

3. Who do you want them to talk to or canvas views from before the session?

4. How do they ask questions or raise any issues they may have before the session?

Consider:

- What information needs to be shared for people to arrive at the workshop ready to participate? That might include a more detailed agenda, clarity of expectations and outcomes, the challenge or generative question to be explored, some contextual positioning for the challenge or topic, or content you will need everyone to refer to and use during the workshop

- What format is best suited to share the information with attendees? E.g. a document to read, a PowerPoint presentation with a script, a webinar briefing video, a personal briefing session for each participant?

- What do you want people to do before attending? This may include questions you want them to consider, other people you want them to talk to in order to represent views from a wide range of stakeholder perspectives, or some reflection questions to prompt their individual meaning-making.

- How, if at all, do you want people to record or share any of their preparation before the workshop? That might include using collaborative platforms like Mural or Jamboard or shared documents on Office SharePoint, OneDrive, Microsoft Teams or Google Docs.

- What kind of technical support will people need? Consider offering a brief technical support session for 10-15 minutes so people are comfortable with the platform you are using before joining the workshop.

- How will you stimulate informal engagement before the workshop? Offer drop-in sessions over coffee to give people a chance to ask any questions about the input, build relationships with other participants, and meet the facilitation team before the workshop. An alternative to this could be a short video message from the facilitation team to all participants introducing themselves and the preparation pack.

Example

I used a number of different preparation approaches for my consulting project that were specific to the audience and the focus of each workshop:

- Co-Creation Workshops: This generative workshop was run multiple times with a different audience each time. Preparation included a slide-based briefing pack, a short video from the CEO, and questions to consider.

- Executive Strategic Session: This was a one-time workshop as part of a longer strategy development project. An individual briefing conversation with each Executive Team member walked them through the outputs from a series of prior stakeholder discovery sessions, a video featuring external experts sharing their views on the strategic topic, and questions for them to consider.

- Harvesting Working Sessions: There were three working sessions attended by the same small group of people. Their purpose was to narrow down the wide range of generative themes created in earlier workshops. To prepare for the first working session, each group member was given a generative theme to discuss with colleagues in their network, and to prepare for the second they tested a series of final options with colleagues in their network.

- Executive Leadership Summit: This was a one-time event attended by executives from five businesses. A series of short briefing videos were created, along with a physical workbook and a self-reflection exercise.

A shift of mindset might be needed when positioning the Frame of Participation to clients and participants so that the Preparation phase is seen as an integral part of the work itself rather than an optional piece of pre-work that will get repeated at the start of a workshop.

A basic workshop flow for a virtual space

There is a generic design flow that forms the foundation for workshops in a virtual space. This sits within the Frame of Participation outlined above and assumes that participants have done some preparation work and are primed for Active Participation.

This design flow may need to be split into two separate sessions depending on the nature of the work being done, as illustrated by the design choice point in *Figure 4* below.

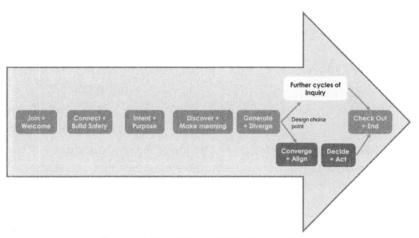

Figure 4 Basic Virtual Workshop Flow

Creating Active Participation in a virtual workshop

Behind the premise of 'Active Participation' is the intent for everyone to engage and contribute as much as possible while attending a virtual workshop so that it is a productive use of time for all. The Active Participation approach is built on the knowledge that there is a limit to the time people can remain engaged, focused, and contributing during a virtual session. While there is little consensus on what is reasonable and possible, I recommend 120 minutes as the maximum time for a productive session. If you want to run a second session on the same day, plan a break of at least 30 minutes before starting the second 90-120 minutes. That gives participants time to step away from the screen, rest their eyes, physically move around, and refresh.

Thoughtfully-designed Active Participation creates psychological safety, builds relationships and bonds between participants. It triggers the release of feel-good hormones that build connection, improve collaboration, and foster teamwork. Virtual workshops need to be designed with a mix of whole-group working, time spent in smaller groups, generating and capturing options, large group work for collective meaning-making and harvesting, and time built in for individual reflection. These can either be structured and facilitated or free-flowing. There are a range of online platforms that have several features that can be included in a design:

1. **Chat**: Ideal for asking people to pose questions, answer a question or contribute to the conversation. When people first join, you can ask them to chat to start to feel part of the group; maybe to say which country or location they are joining from, to share what drink they have at their desk, to volunteer what they are hoping to get out of attending or share a burning question related to the topic for the workshop.

   • You can also set up paired discussions by asking people to use 'private chat' with a nominated person to discuss a question or explore a topic.

   • You can use Chat as a check-in point during a workshop to find out what people are finding beneficial, how they could use what's been introduced (if it's a learning session), how the pace is working for them, or how they are feeling now.

   • There are more ways to use Chat in Chapter 4.

2. **Reactions**: These simple emojis are a quick and easy way to build interaction, engagement and give you instant feedback.

3. **Breakout rooms**: To divide the group into smaller groups. See Chapter 4 for more information on designing and using breakout rooms.

4. **Whiteboards**: To capture conversations and ideas either in the large group or in breakout rooms.

5. **Polls**: To check understanding, gain feedback, and assist with decision making. Polls enable participants to vote on a series of options or indicate their levels of commitment to a proposal. External platforms like Mentimeter also provide this.

6. **Annotate**: To add comments, symbols, or vote on a document/slide being shared.

7. **Gallery View/Speaker View**: On the leading platforms of Zoom and Microsoft Teams, there are options to adjust the layout and size of the video windows on the screen. On Zoom, you can either enable 'Gallery View' (where everyone is seen in the same size rectangular boxes) or 'Speaker View' (where the person speaking is shown larger than those not speaking).

8. **Video recording**: Depending on the conversations' sensitivity and how the content will be used, you can record the discussions. That can be done either through the platform you are using or an external software app like Otter, which automatically transcribes the conversations into a written document. It is essential to check that everyone is OK for this to happen, that no commercially-sensitive content is inappropriately recorded, and that storage of the recording is secure. You may find that some participants contribute less if they are unsure who will have access to the recording.

9. **Collaborative Platforms**: Many collaborative platforms allow for synchronous and asynchronous working, making idea generation visible to everyone simultaneously (Mural, Miro, Google Suite, etc.). These can be effectively used during the Preparation phase as well as during the workshop itself—more of this in Chapter 4. If you want to incorporate using these, it is a simple case of posting the link into Chat or sending it out with the Preparation information.

Example:
I kept the technology really simple in the early stages of working with a client, using only the basic functions on the Zoom platform we used. This was due to a number of factors: a culture of on-site working and face-to-face meetings, inexperience of collaborative working between businesses, restricted access to shared platforms, accessibility restrictions due to poor internet connection, and low-specification IT equipment for home working. As the project progressed, people's confidence increased as they attended more work meetings online, their knowledge and familiarity with the Zoom platform grew, and they got to know each other more. As a result, towards the end of the project I was able to introduce more advanced features.

A word of caution: It's very tempting to use everything that your chosen online platform can do right from the start by 'showing off' all the bells and whistles. This can result in clients feeling a little overawed with the technology if it is new to them and worried about not getting things right. That can lead to discussions focusing more on the technology and less on the contributions you want them to make.

Summary of key points from this chapter

- Reframing the concept of participation is one of the key changes needed when designing and hosting workshops online.

- Our concentration span is less when we are online, and we get tired quickly. As a result, virtual workshops need to be shorter to keep us engaged.

- To help participants arrive at a workshop ready to contribute, widen the Frame of Participation by designing a series of Preparation activities before the workshop.

- Preparation can include short videos, questions to answer, and briefing documents. These will get participants ready for Active Participation at the workshop.

Designing Virtual Spaces

This chapter shares design principles that inform decisions regarding the type and shape of container needed in a virtual space, from the 'birds' eye' overview of a program arc to the detailed design of a workshop session. Four distinct design options are introduced that can be sequenced in multiple ways to create a tailored program arc for a client. The second half of the chapter explores how the maturity levels for virtual working within an organization impact our virtual designs.

In Dialogic OD we are rarely designing a single standalone workshop. Much of our work involves creating a sequence of interventions, working with our clients to select the appropriate type and shape of the containers, and deciding the pace and frequency needed in service of our client system.

Design principles and four kinds of virtual containers

Successful workshops live or die on participant engagement levels, and this doesn't change in a virtual space. In fact, due to everything we know about attention spans, it seems even more critical. Designing interactive and engaging processes for online workshops needs careful consideration to avoid participants becoming bored or distracted by other work on their screens. Here are some approaches to help build engagement and interaction into your design:

- Design for connection before content, allow sufficient time in the design to build relationships and for participants to connect with each other.

- Keep sessions short and focused using the design frameworks above.

- Limit the use of presentations and 'talking heads' by incorporating this into the Preparation phase of the Frame of Participation. That ensures people are ready for Active Participation.

- Agree on ground rules at the start that address and limits other distractions, both on and off computer screens.

- Design for inclusion—consider issues of accessibility and inclusivity in your design.

- Use a wide variety of interactive processes and breakout rooms.

As I begin designing an OD process, these four design principles shape the program arc of my work. These are relevant for both physical place and virtual space—it is the way they are brought to life that is different.

1. **Context:** What is happening in the broader system that impacts and connects to this work?

2. **Business outcomes:** What business outcomes are this work in service of? What has triggered the need for this work to be done?

3. **Human experience:** What human experience are we creating or disrupting? What human development do we want to incorporate into our design?

4. **Relational dynamics:** What are the relational dynamics in the system that we need to pay attention to?

Depending on the purpose of your virtual space, and the organizational outcomes you may be generating, you can configure a program arc that considers and incorporates one or more of the following:

- A system-wide perspective.

- A transformation program.

- A series of linked interventions and containers.

- A single standalone event/workshop.

There's only so much people can take in and process while working in a virtual space, and the psychological impacts of virtual working mean that we need to consider how best to sequence and design virtual workshops.

It isn't as simple as a direct transfer of the design of a day's physical workshop to a day's workshop online. How you decide to use the duration and sequencing of workshops can create different experiences, different levels of intensity, different ways to support key activities in a wider piece of organizational work, and generate pace and momentum for action.

One of the dilemmas is, do you do more sessions in quick succession, or do you spread things out over several sessions to give people time in-between to reflect or act and experiment?

You may find that designing for virtual spaces takes more time than face-to-face workshops, at least initially, as you develop your own approaches to incorporate different design options for the workshop itself, along with the range of Preparation activities that need to be planned and created.

Four design containers

Here I have simplified the design options available to you into four distinct types, each with a specific intent.

1. **Focus:** this is the most straightforward design option, a single session lasting between 60-120 minutes. 'Focus' sessions are best used for a single topic or activity, and can be supplemented with more 'focus' sessions designed into the program arc to build momentum and a pattern. Daily or weekly 'focus' sessions can create an underlying rhythm or drumbeat within a transformation project.

2. **Deepen:** this design option has multiple sessions running on the same day, these sessions can vary in length but all have a substantial break between them. By running multiple sessions in the same day you can cover a number of related topics, get under the skin of a particular topic, or flesh out a series of options that are generated. The 'deepen' design option creates an intensity which can build relationships and accelerate team working

3. **Soak:** these sessions are used when you want to give participants time to absorb and reflect on what has been covered. They are great spaces in between a series of workshops for individual 'digestion' to take place, where complex topics or prompted reflection questions encourage people to search inwards for meaning making. They are a

powerful way of slowing the system down before moving to decision making.

4. **Network:** the final design option also creates an intentional gap between sessions. This gap creates the opportunity for participants to reach out across their networks, or to specific stakeholder groups. This is to conduct a pre-agreed inquiry, or test out proposed options, to gain insights and a wider range of perspectives to inform what happens next.

Table 3 summarizes the four design options to consider when creating a program of interventions.

Table 3 Design options for Virtual OD

Design Option	Suggested duration	Features and Benefits
Focus A single session	• 60-90-120 minutes with one or two short breaks	• The session is contained within one day • There is a limit to how much can be covered • A rhythm can be created with daily or weekly sessions of equal length, held at the same time each day/week. This can build focus and increase momentum
Deepen Multiple sessions that take place within a day	• Two or three 90-minute sessions with a break after 45 minutes • A longer break between each session of c30-40 minutes	• The session is contained within one day • There is a lot covered in one day • The work can become relationally deeper • Concentrates and focuses attention • Builds momentum • Can be intense for participants

Design Option	Suggested duration	Features and Benefits
Soak A series of sessions that takes place with gaps in between to absorb and reflect	• Up to two 90-minute sessions on one day • A gap of between 5-10 days primed with an individual reflection question • The timeframe for soaking and reflecting can vary depending on the nature of the work and outcomes required • A second or third series of 90-minute sessions	• Participants have time to absorb and soak in the topics discussed • A question at the close of a session takes participants into a deeper level of reflection, or consideration • The next session begins with a collective reflection session based on what has emerged • Useful with complex situations and for those who are natural reflectors • Slows down those who like to jump to solution • Encourages considered contributions from all voices
Network A series of sessions that prime people to conduct specific inquiry conversations or agreed on experiments between each session and return with new insights from across a wider system	• One or two 90-minute sessions on one day • A gap of 5+ days with specific inquiry questions to be explored with key stakeholders inside/outside the business, or with small teams. The gap will depend on the nature and reach of the inquiry, who is involved, and the momentum that needs to be built or maintained	• Good for longer-term transformation work • Builds a rhythm within a business, keeping transformative conversations visible and alive • Balances divergence and generative thinking with convergence and narrowing down • Extends the circle of involvement and engagement • Encourages the system to self-diagnose and self-generate • Insights from inquiry questions bring back new data and insights. These, in turn, inform what happens next • Experiments are undertaken to test out what might happen —intended and unintended consequences

Design Option	Suggested duration	Features and Benefits
Network (continued)	• Experimenting with new behaviors or testing out ways of working • A further 90-minute session to share insights and generate new inquiry questions or experiments as required Continue to repeat the pattern of inquiry and re-group sessions as many times as required	• Builds relationships and networks across the system and can be used to increase collaboration between departments or organizations • Builds energy for and commitment to change • Multiple cycles of multiple inquiries can create pockets of pattern disturbance across a system

The detailed design for each of these options will always incorporate the Frame of Participation covered in Chapter 2, with whatever preparation is appropriate.

Depending on the program arc you are designing, you can consider which combination, frequency, and sequencing of these design options produce the pace and results that will best deliver the Dialogic OD work's intention. Each of the design choices has an impact on the human experience and relational dynamics.

Figure 5 gives a visual example of a program arc created using a combination of the four different approaches in a sequence. You may not always have all four approaches in a program.

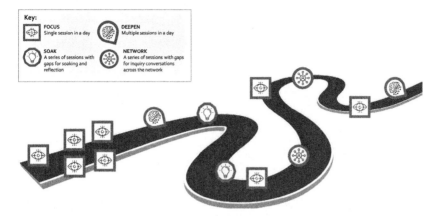

Figure 5 Combining and sequencing containers to create a program arc

Maturity levels for virtual working

It is important to meet the client organization where they are comfortable working and collaborating in a virtual space, rather than introducing too many variables from the start.

There are many sophisticated apps and tools that can enhance and introduce different ways of interacting, generating, and capturing outputs as they occur in virtual spaces. These introduce variety and can be fun for the participant, and all have their place.

If too many unfamiliar platforms and features are introduced at once this can create anxiety and hinder participation and contribution. There is a relationship between the level of maturity and mindset in an organization regarding how they view collaborative virtual working and how willing they are to embrace different tools and platforms introduced to them in workshops.

Figure 6 shows three levels of maturity and mindset you may see that indicate where an organization is on this scale.

This will impact the choices you make about design and hosting, and how you pace the introduction of new technology and virtual platforms.

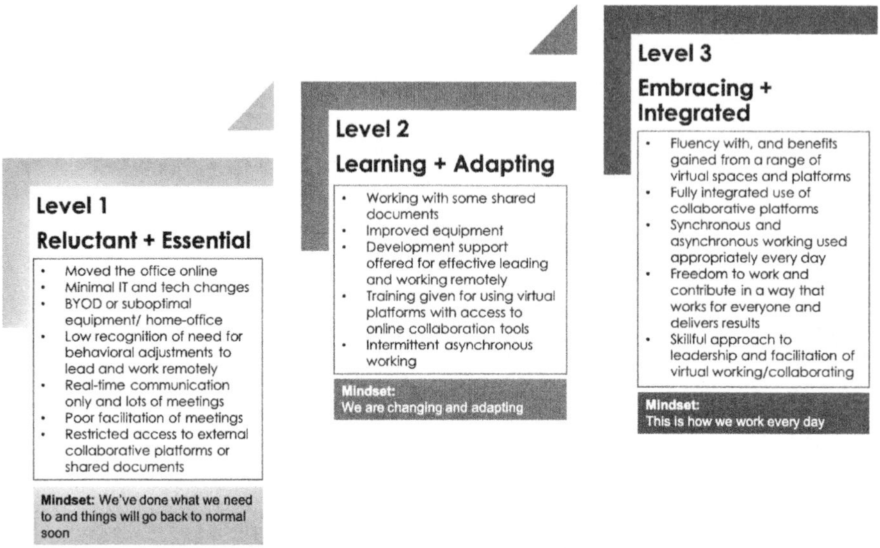

Level 1

Reluctant + Essential

- Moved the office online
- Minimal IT and tech changes
- BYOD or suboptimal equipment/ home-office
- Low recognition of need for behavioral adjustments to lead and work remotely
- Real-time communication only and lots of meetings
- Poor facilitation of meetings
- Restricted access to external collaborative platforms or shared documents

Mindset: We've done what we need to and things will go back to normal soon

Level 2

Learning + Adapting

- Working with some shared documents
- Improved equipment
- Development support offered for effective leading and working remotely
- Training given for using virtual platforms with access to online collaboration tools
- Intermittent asynchronous working

Mindset:
We are changing and adapting

Level 3

Embracing + Integrated

- Fluency with, and benefits gained from a range of virtual spaces and platforms
- Fully integrated use of collaborative platforms
- Synchronous and asynchronous working used appropriately every day
- Freedom to work and contribute in a way that works for everyone and delivers results
- Skilful approach to leadership and facilitation of virtual working/collaborating

Mindset:
This is how we work every day

Figure 6: Organization maturity levels for virtual working

Example:

Five organizations I worked with were all at Level I on this maturity scale. There was little use of virtual platforms, and nothing that could be accessed by all organizations within the group. They were unfamiliar with Zoom as a platform, and had inconsistencies with gaining access to the internet from their home, and were working on a range of devices—laptops, phones and iPads.

This limited the range of options I could incorporate into the workshop designs. As a result I needed to keep the session design short and simple, with preparation work that could be downloaded easily on different kinds of devices. I used the 'focus' design for the initial generative workshops, and only used two Zoom features so participants didn't feel overwhelmed or confused. The number of participants was kept low so technical support could be offered during the session. This meant that multiple sessions had to be run in a short period of time in order to engage the number of employees needed.

This Level I maturity also showed up as an initial hesitation to engage in virtual working as it was seen as a temporary arrangement and a sub-optimal way of working. By the end of the assignment they were moving rapidly towards Level 2; commenting on how enjoyable and productive working virtually was for them, and introducing shared platforms and collaborative hubs into the businesses. If that project started now, I would have a much greater range of options to draw from to create the program arc, and a more open and willing participant mindset to work with.

Summary of key points from this chapter

- The design of a program arc needs to account for context, business outcome, human experience and relational dynamics.

- There are four basic design options to create a virtual program arc: Focus, Deepen, Soak, and Network. Each of these generates a different rhythm and pace across a program and enables a wide range of stakeholders to contribute.

- The virtual working maturity level of the organization provides a helpful guide for the appropriate use of technology platforms and features in your design.

FOUR

Mastering Technology

This chapter discusses the importance of being familiar with the technology you are using. It also outlines the key features available on virtual platforms and the best ways to incorporate them into virtual designs to generate high levels of participant engagement and interaction. The chapter covers ways to build participation and interaction synchronously (done live, together) and asynchronously (done on your own time), and explore some of what is different with virtual interactions.

Familiarization with the technology

Feeling confident and comfortable using the different features of your chosen technical platform makes a huge difference to the experience you create for participants. I cannot emphasize enough the need to practice and rehearse the critical elements of your design and the transitions between each section with a co-facilitator or colleague.

The technical considerations are hugely different from those in a physical place and present a key choice: how much to do as a solo facilitator, and at what point you bring in a co-facilitator and/or a technical facilitator. Virtual facilitation often requires spinning multiple plates. While this is doable by someone skilled with the technical platform and the workshop's content, every extra layer of technical complexity you add creates the possibility of stress or mistakes.

You may need to figure out how to replicate a workshop process you might use in a face-to-face workshop and reconfigure it for a virtual session. Here is an example:

Imagine how you might have run a series of generative conversations across a number of breakout sessions during a co-creation workshop.

This is where small groups contribute and build on each other's ideas, circulating around the room as if on a carousel. If I were physically in that room, I'd be saying: '*Each group grab a piece of flipchart paper and go to these four working stations around the room. Capture the outputs of your conversations and ideas onto the flipchart, then move clockwise around the room to the next flipchart. Over the next 30 minutes, keep rotating round until you've visited each flipchart.*'

Example:

The 'virtual carousel' is one of the approaches I used in the design of a series of generative workshops. The workshop ran multiple times for groups of 12-15 people across five different businesses, capturing the contributions of 600+ people. This was during the early stages of the project and I chose to adopt a simple process for capturing and sharing outputs generated by each breakout group during the 'virtual carousel' session.

People were inexperienced in virtual collaboration and had restricted access to external platforms on their computer, in addition I didn't want a fear of technology to be a barrier to people's contribution. We used a simple capturing template on a PowerPoint slide that was saved onto the computer of one group member, then re-shared by uploading the slide into the Chat box at the end of each round of the carousel.

To do that in a virtual space, as a 'virtual carousel', there are several technical elements that need to happen:

- Using breakout rooms: working out who's going into which room, allocating them to those rooms, making sure they know how to accept the link to join the room.

- Capturing outputs: deciding how to create and build a live document (the virtual flipchart) to capture each group's outputs, and agreeing on how that document moves between groups in each of the rooms. **In a virtual space, the document (the virtual flipchart) moves around each group, rather than each group moving to a new flipchart.** There are a few different ways you can capture these outputs: on a document that gets saved each time and re-shared to the next group if you are taking a simplified approach, via a shared document housed on a central platform, or on an external collaborative platform.

- Supporting the groups—being available, or supplying additional scribes to help the group capture their outputs, rather than being overly concerned about getting the technical stuff right.

Technical features and tools to incorporate into your design:

Using Chat

Chat is a useful way to incorporate high levels of interactivity into a session design. Chat can be used to:

1. Build connection and safety: participants can be asked to introduce themselves and disclose information through Chat. This can be low intensity—where they work, their role, where they live, what drink they have in their mug—and then deepen with greater disclosure levels.

2. Generate ground rules for group behavior and agree on how the Chat function will be used, e.g. to ask questions, make observations, contribute to discussions, etc.

3. It can feel safer to contribute via Chat in a large group. If the group is large, and you want to create some interaction without going into breakout rooms, then a paired conversation via private chat can become a safe space to explore perspectives.

4. Generate ideas and options.

5. Share themes from conversations in smaller groups, allowing others to see what was discussed without needing a full report-back from each group.

6. Ask questions during a session, or request for all questions to be logged into Chat at a particular point in the session. This enables the host to see the range of questions and respond accordingly.

7. Provide a silent, reflective space for everyone to contribute. Just as in face-to-face workshops, some people want to contribute without speaking.

8. Comment live in Chat on what is being discussed in the session. This can be distracting for some but can also provide a rich discussion across a large group in a way that a conversation couldn't do. This commentary can be analyzed for themes and then shared back with the group later to aid learning about the group working process.

9. Check out opinions on a proposed solution.

10. Vote on a decision.

11. Gather data to help move a group forward.

12. Give feedback on a session. One technique is a Chat Storm, where everyone is asked the same question, for example, 'What is the thing I valued most from this session?'. Everyone writes their answers but doesn't post the answer until instructed. The Chat box is then flooded with responses that everyone can pause to read together.

13. Share a reflection, a learning, or a takeaway, at the end of a session. This can be creatively done in a 'Reflection Relay'. In groups of three, the first of the trio writes a private message to the second person sharing one piece of learning or a takeaway from the session. The second person adds their learning/takeaway and sends it to the third person, who adds their learning/takeaway and then posts the whole message to everyone. There is a sudden burst of Chat clusters that share multiple learning and takeaways from a session.

Some tips to help manage Chat live in a session

- Encourage people to use Chat right from the beginning of a session. It's a quick and simple way to get interaction and engagement.

- Build pause points into your design where you refer to Chat, or ask your co-host to summarize themes or respond to questions.

- Ask people to annotate their contributions before they write their Chat message. Q – question, O – observation, or C – comment. That makes it easier as a host or co-host to spot and respond.

- As a host, put a line of dashes in Chat to separate different topics and help you spot comments or questions that you have already attended to.

The whole Chat record from a workshop can be saved and downloaded by any participant at the end if that function is enabled on the platform. In Zoom, Chat doesn't save breakout room conversations and only captures the private chat the person downloading may have had with others. It doesn't capture all the private chats that have taken place during the workshop unless they were sent to that person.

Using breakout rooms

There are different ways of dividing a large group into smaller working groups depending on which online platform you are using. On Zoom and MS Teams, this is done with breakout rooms. Working in smaller groups is a compelling way of engaging participants in deeper conversations. You can use and run these in several ways on both platforms. Here we look at the features on Zoom:

1. To discuss a common question in small groups and have the responses reported back to the main group. You can write the question in the Chat box so everyone can see it, or ask them to note it down. If it is more than one question or complex, you can put a link in the Chat box to a URL where you have previously uploaded the document.

2. For each group to discuss a different question.

    1. There are two ways to do this, the first just stays within the Zoom platform. You can mimic a generative session with flipcharts around a room where people build on each other's contributions and then share their responses back in the main group. To do this, write the question or upload a briefing slide into Chat (This is done by clicking on 'file' in the Chat box, and then uploading the document from your computer system). Participants then download the slide onto their computer, and someone in the group captures the output on behalf of their group, saves the slide and then shares it back in the main group by uploading it via Chat once everyone is out of the breakout rooms.

2. The second way to do this involves accessing platforms outside Zoom. To do this, everyone works on a shared document, like a Google doc, that can be generated and developed whilst in breakout rooms. The document is visible to everyone on the call and makes sharing outputs from each group much easier.

3. As host, you can select who goes into each breakout room and for how long. Once the breakout room time ends, everyone returns to the 'main group' automatically, unless as host you choose to keep the room open longer.

4. Participants need to follow the prompts to join the breakout room they have been invited to, and they will see a 30 or 60 second countdown to show that the breakout room will shortly close. You can have a countdown timer displayed, so people know exactly how long they have left in the breakout room.

5. There is also an option for participants to select which breakout room they want to join. Depending on the nature of the workshop you are running, you may want to invite them to do this.

6. The host can broadcast a message to all rooms. This can be a helpful reminder for specific actions that need to be completed before the breakout room session ends. On Zoom, these can sometimes be missed, so it's good to warn the groups you may be sending a message near the end of the session.

7. As hosts and co-hosts, you can circulate around the breakout rooms to join in or check out how the group are progressing, offering support if needed. Co-hosts cannot move around until they have been sent to one breakout room by the host. There are two ways to handle this: one is to create a separate Host Room and move yourselves in and out of any of the rooms from there. A Host Room is useful to have for the hosting team to meet privately as needed. The other way is for the hosting team to stay in the main room and have the host send co-hosts to the first room they want to visit.

8. The meeting host should stay in the main room in case participants need help or exit the meeting and need to be let back in. Participants can return to the main room at any time or send a message to the host to ask for help or support.

9. If your event/workshop is a long one, create a 'Chillout room' where participants can go for some time-out if they want to and connect with others informally. If they need some time alone, then they can step away from their computer screen.

Capturing and recording outputs

There are many different ways to capture conversations and outputs from a workshop. The simplest way is to record the workshop (audio or video) and place it somewhere where it can be accessed by everyone who attended—password protected if required. That way everyone has access to the verbal conversations that took place.

To capture conversation outputs visually there are tools incorporated within the virtual meeting platforms themselves, some are on operating systems like Microsoft 365 and Google, and others are accessed through separate apps. Whiteboards on Zoom are only visible while accessing the platform during a workshop and need to be saved before exiting, while others are cloud-based and can be accessed at any time, on any device.

All of the visual capturing options have different features and plus points. The choice of which one to use may be a personal one or governed by your client and the systems they use. Either way, consider the maturity levels of online working that exist in the organization.

If there are any restrictions on using external applications and documents, then a straightforward approach can have a host/notetaker record off the screen and share at intervals during the session. That also releases any pressure or anxiety that participants may feel about making mistakes or 'getting it wrong', and allow them to focus on contributing.

Some of the more popular tools are:

- Virtual whiteboards within Zoom, Microsoft Teams and on Jamboard in Google Suite.

- Shared collaborative platforms with live documents on Google Drive or Microsoft 365 where Word, PowerPoint or Excel documents can be generated and edited live.

- Visual collaborative workspaces—the commons ones are Mural and Mira, although there are many more available. These can be used to create visual shared spaces for generative sessions, and to capture other dialogue outputs.

The shared collaborative platforms and workspaces can be incorporated into a design in two different ways:

Synchronous working

Shared documents or collaborative workspaces allow groups and teams to work with these tools simultaneously. Participants can capture their work, work with others to generate ideas, and collaboratively build on others' contributions in a visible and accessible way for everyone while the working session is taking place.

Asynchronous Working

Asynchronous working activities on collaborative platforms (where everyone works on the same document at different times) can be incorporated into separate stages of a workshop design:

Preparation phase: Individuals can participate in preparation activities and post any initial ideas and contributions onto an allocated space on a Mural board or Google document.

- If participants are new to using these kinds of platforms, some simple instructions or an accompanying video can help build confidence.

- Activities to get to know each other and build trust can feature in this phase. These include inviting participants to post photographs or images of different aspects of their life or responding to a series of 'get to know you' questions.

- You can assign people to pre-work groups, asking them to explore questions or topics to gather themes for meaning-making at the workshop.

- It can be helpful to set out clearly-identified working spaces or use pre-generated templates with some starting inputs.

Active Participation: During a workshop, the outputs from the preparation work can be developed or used as inquiry data.

- Breakout groups can continue to populate separate sections of a collaborative document during the workshop.

- Reporting back from each group is accelerated as people see the work of that group and hear the summary.

Example:

The design of a mini-series of workshops adopted the Focus design approach with a single session each week for three consecutive weeks. The program arc was collaboratively designed by a small team of four people, with pairs co-creating the detailed design of each individual session. We used Mural as our collaborative platform and created a series of Mural boards for the program arc itself, and for each separate workshop.

We worked asynchronously and synchronously at different stages of the design process. Each of us was able to work at a time and pace that accommodated other priorities and quickly see how each workshop design was progressing as often as we wished. We created a rhythm of short weekly meetings to share, inform, and gather feedback/ideas for the next iteration of design.

Attendees were invited to join a Preparation board and form pairs to have a conversation, the themes and outputs from which were captured under different sections on the board. For some it was their first-time using Mural, so simple instructions were shared, and people encouraged to experiment.

Each workshop was designed to use different features available on the Zoom platform, and incorporated outputs from the Preparation work to inform conversations and discussions. The outputs of the first workshop informed the second, and so on.

Synchronous and asynchronous working was used during and after each workshop, and outputs from each individual workshop were harvested, themed, and used to inform follow-up action after the mini-series concluded.

Follow Up: After a workshop has ended, the collaborative document can be used in many ways:

- A visual record of the workshop can become part of the documented narrative or data set for the next phase of an assignment.

- A place for continued contribution, reflection, or feedback— either alone or with small action groups.

- A way to inform and engage other stakeholders with the work through continued rounds of exploration, generation, and shared meaning-making.

Using collaborative documents and platforms in this way creates a connected flow throughout a single workshop or series of workshops. The choices as to how and when to incorporate these into a design depend on the workshop's outcomes.

Consideration for a program arc

At a meta-level, consideration needs to be given to the overall information and data requirements across an intervention: what it is needed for, how it will be shared, which elements of the program arc need connecting, and what decision points it will inform. This will then guide decisions on the best way to generate, capture, store, and share. Each of these synchronous and asynchronous approaches are valuable when working collaboratively with consulting colleagues too.

What's different with virtual workshops and events?

Conversation flow is different

Cross-talking or stilted conversation flow can be a challenge in even the best designed and hosted virtual space. Participating in online workshops lacks many of the nonverbal cues we give off and receive when physically present. These are the cues that allow us to calibrate and know when and how to reply and join an ongoing conversation. Conversations can also be impacted by technical issues like poor internet connection and sound quality or the sheer size of the group.

Ways to counteract these include:

- Getting people to write their questions in Chat so you can get a sense of the range of questions and cluster them together into themes to respond to.

- Asking open questions that people discuss in pairs or small groups first, to encourage quieter people to contribute to the larger group.

- Splitting a large group into small breakout rooms, with sufficient time for everyone to contribute, helps to manage conversation flow.

- Requesting brief contributions or 'one breath' comments. This is where the speaker can only talk as long as one breath lasts; they can't continue to speak once they need to retake a breath. It can also be a fun way to balance contributions and pay attention to what people are saying.

- As the host, you can invite people to speak, or ask the person speaking to nominate the next person.

- There are different views on whether microphones should be on or off during a workshop or event. For smaller groups I like to encourage people to leave them on as it builds a greater sense of intimacy and the group soon learn how to balance their contributions. For larger groups it may be better to ask people to stay on mute unless they are speaking. There isn't a 'right' or 'wrong' approach to this, and I would encourage you to experiment with different groups depending on the nature of your work and the outcomes you are working towards.

- Build different approaches into your design that increase participation—individual work, paired chat conversations, poll voting, annotating whiteboards, and so on.

- Different conversation flows occur in groups who haven't worked together before, so taking time for everyone to contribute at the start will build safety, confidence and trust.

There can be a loss of liminal space and collective energy

There's something visceral and powerful about the energy, noise and hubbub that goes on when you are in a room with many people—it resonates in our bodies. The underlying hum of conversation draws us in and generates a curiosity when you can see people huddled in small groups having conversations. If you were to hover over a room during a lunch break or an extended coffee break, you would see patterns of fluid movement and connection as temporary groups form and split up as people move around.

We lose the chance to have serendipitous conversations with someone new in the coffee break or lunch line in a virtual workshop or event. We lose the ability to bump into a friend or colleague on the way into a workshop, or share our reflections in the social networking spaces at the end of the day.

These valuable informal interactions are lost unless they are consciously built into the design, and even then, these can feel a bit engineered. Lots of important stuff happens outside of the formal sessions, so we need to recreate people's ability to informally network, make meaning in that space, and build relationships. These informal spaces build safety, connection, and relationships, which are important in the dialogic approach to transformation.

A thoughtful design can replicate some of those spaces through creating 'connection breakout rooms' before a workshop starts—putting a few people into breakout rooms for 10 minutes so they can have a bit of a chat with whoever's there as they would over coffee at the start of a workshop. An informal virtual 'cocktail party' or 'wine tasting' at the end of a working session can create a social space for people to decompress.

> At an online event with 70+ attendees from different organizations we used 'connection breakout rooms' at the start. As attendees arrived they were admitted into the meeting in groups, welcomed, and then placed into breakout rooms in groups of four. They remained in those rooms for 10 minutes to get to know each other, and then switched to a second group with new people for a further 10 minutes, and then a third, before coming together as a whole group.

These in-between spaces I've described are known as *liminal spaces*. They are defined as being a boundary or threshold between one thing and another (Denham-Vaughan, 2010). They are spaces we move through physically and psychologically. In physical dialogic places, we create a clear 'transition space'; the moment where one working session ends and the act of physically moving out of a room or building to a different space takes place. These transition spaces are important for our reflection and allow us to digest what has taken place.

When we work in virtual spaces, these transition spaces are lost. When we click 'Leave Meeting', we are instantly cut off from those we have spent time with. If we have invested something of ourselves in building deeper relationships with colleagues, or become more vulnerable by revealing something about ourselves, raising a difficult topic or challenging something we hold a different perspective on, this transition can be jarring, causing what Brene Brown (2010) calls a 'vulnerability hangover'. Our home or office life crashes in when we exit a virtual workshop, interrupting the liminal digestion space that allows us to calibrate and chat with colleagues to minimize a vulnerability hangover or just to absorb and adjust before moving on to the next thing.

Example:

At the end of client workshops where I was running multiple sessions I often stayed online for 10-15 minutes to allow those who wanted to stay and chat to do so. Those who stayed, sometimes asked a question, but more often they chatted through something that was raised during the workshop or shared an observation on the culture of the business that might impact the next stage of the work we were doing. These liminal space conversations frequently gave me insights into what was happening that I wouldn't have gained during the workshop. This 'liminal' decompression space replicated the time I would spend tidying up the workshop room, sorting out flipcharts and packing things up. It seemed to offer a transition space to participants and elicit contributions or observations they didn't feel able to share in the session

Summary of key points from this chapter

- Incorporate plenty of interaction into your workshop as early as possible, using the key features like Chat, Polls, and Breakout Rooms.

- Incorporate a blend of synchronous and asynchronous working on collaborative platforms into your designs; they can be especially impactful during the Preparation stage and accelerate a sense of connection in a group.

- To keep participants engaged and contributing, incorporate different features from your virtual platform into your design. Don't overwhelm with too much technology if people aren't used to it.

- Where possible work with a co-host and technical host.

FIVE

Hosting with Presence

This chapter explores aspects of how we use our presence as hosts to support the group or team's work online. I explore a range of hosting roles and share some of the critical differences that impact our virtual presence. The chapter closes by looking at ways in which we can create psychological safety online for participants to be able to contribute fully.

Our hosting space

The space where we apply our craft and skills as a host or facilitator has radically changed, and as a result, we have to think differently about our presence and impact. What was once a three-dimensional workshop room filled with chairs, tables, projector, screens, flipcharts, chisel-tip marker pens, and other associated 'kit' has now become a grid of rect-angles within a rectangle. Our computer screen is filled with a uniform grid of boxes with a head and shoulders view of people in neat rows. Gone is the space to move around, to 'work the room', to draw groups of people into corners with flipcharts on the wall. This is replaced by Gallery View, Speaker View, Chat, Breakout Rooms, Pin Video, Share Screen, Mute, Polls, and Online Collaboration Tools.

We now apply ourselves in this two-dimensional world to support the work of our client systems.

Personal presence

Our online presence can feel more and less intimate at the same time because of our physical proximity to the screen and each other. We 'see' people in a way that we don't normally when we are sitting in a circle or around a table. We see them head-on, rather than a range of partial or side views of people's bodies and faces. I can switch between Speaker View and Gallery View to either see the person speaking or everyone as a whole group. If I want to focus on one person, I can 'Pin video' to continue to see them even as others are talking.

Hosting with presence in virtual space changes many dynamics that we are used to noticing when we are physically in a room together. We turn up by logging on to our virtual space and then make a series of choices as to what we do next that create our presence and impact in a virtual space.

Adjusting our presence in a virtual space

At a simple level, three elements are building blocks for our presence in a virtual space:

1. **How we look:** What people see of us when we have our camera on: our proximity to the screen, having the camera angled to show our head and shoulders, having our face lit, whether we sit or stand, what can be seen behind us in our 'Zoom zone' or if we use a backdrop, which backdrop we choose, and the clothes we wear to match or disrupt the organizational norms.

2. **How we sound:** Our voice tonality, pitch, pace, volume, and whether we wear a headset, use a separate microphone, or use the computer camera/speakers/microphone.

3. **How we fill our space:** Our ability to connect and communicate: making eye contact and 'seeing' everyone; how much we move around physically, and how still we are to provide a calm and reassuring presence, how we show we are listening, the choices we make about what we say, and when we say it.

Below is an aspect of each of these that I've used to adjust my presence since working in virtual spaces, plus an exercise to gauge your virtual presence that you can complete with colleagues.

Sharing Slides

I try to limit the amount I use slides during an online session, sharing any input needed via a video recording or a reading/information pack in the Preparation stage beforehand.

Depending on the audience, I sometimes conduct a 1:1 briefing session with all participants if critical content needs to be assimilated or explored. This also has benefits for building key relationships and developing understanding.

When slides are shared on virtual platforms, the screen configuration is changed and the slides take over the screen, and the view of you as presenter shrinks. This is the case even when participants select 'Speaker View'. To overcome this, the few slides I use are focused on key points only or to brief an exercise. Anything more complicated gets covered differently, either during the Preparation stage or spread over a number of sessions.

There are two things you can do to adjust the balance between you and your slides on screen, both of which require you to use a green screen or other virtual backgrounds:

1. Create a photograph of each slide and upload them as virtual backgrounds. You move through to the next slide by changing your virtual background. If there are many participants attending it can help if you 'Spotlight' yourself so your image is 'locked' as the largest on the screen, that will enable participants to easily see what's written on your virtual background.

2. If you are using Zoom, there is an advanced tab on the 'Share Screen' menu. Here you can select 'Slides As Background', which opens up your presentation as the virtual background behind you. You move through the slides in the same way as you would a standard presentation. You can move your image around the screen and resize it to be larger or smaller.

Headsets and Microphones

Even something as simple as using a headset and microphone impacts presence. These can be a headset/microphone combined or separate pieces. Here are some reasons why I use one:

- I feel more connected to everyone and can hear other people more clearly.

- It's respectful to those listening—a signal that you and what you say are important to me.

- It can improve the sound quality for others on the call.

- Creates a safe space and privacy—other people can't overhear the conversation.

- Enables me to focus on what I'm doing: removing distracting sounds for me and others.

- Voice tonality and pace: I can speak normally and not strain my voice, and I can access a wider range of voice tonality that is more easily heard. Varying my voice tone and pace can create more intimacy, building trust and safety.

- There are mixed views about whether microphones should be continuously left off or muted when people aren't speaking. There are some situations when there is better connection and dialogue when people aren't muting themselves, the conversation can feel more natural and people adjust to working in that way. Where it's not possible to reduce background noise and distractions then muting can work well and should be suggested.

Eye contact

Eye contact is one way we connect with people, and making direct eye contact is impossible with current video and camera configurations. We don't know if someone is looking at us and connecting with us, nor is it easy to pick up signals that reassure us they hear what we say.

There are ways to create a sense of connection and make eye contact with someone by adjusting how we use the camera and move our eyes:

- Switch off Self View so you are not being distracted by continually looking at yourself on the screen. It is amazing how distracting this can be. When you are next in a virtual session, notice how often you are looking at yourself rather than everyone else on the call.

- Place the Zoom window as close to the top of your screen as possible. This will bring it near the camera so that when you are looking at the window, it appears that you are looking at the camera.

- I advise you not to stare continuously into the camera—as some people suggest—because this is the equivalent of 'staring' at someone. If we continually stare at the camera, we miss the visual cues participants' expressions and body language are giving us; this is important data we need to adjust our response. When we speak in real life, our gaze moves around someone's face; we don't stare at their eyes all the time.

- We can replicate that 'soft gaze' by moving from looking into the camera to gently looking at someone's eyes, and gaze around their face before returning to the camera again. The movement needs to be relaxed and slow for it to feel natural and authentic.

Adjusting my presence

It's been invaluable for me to discover the impact my presence has on others when I'm hosting online. Here's a short exercise you may want to try with colleagues that also sharpens our ability to articulate what we notice and share with others. Please pay attention to how you create a safe space for this work and how you each set and honor boundaries of what gets discussed:

Working with a small group (four or five) people

- Individually consider the three or four 'signature' hallmarks of your presence when hosting or facilitating face to face.

- Think about how these translate into a virtual space and what you might want to get feedback on—either things to amplify or dampen.

- Contract with the group for the kind of feedback you want, e.g. your voice, how well you can be seen, what your presence evokes, suggestions to improve your online presence.

- Speak uninterrupted for 60-90 seconds about what you love about your work.

- After you've spoken, each person gives you brief feedback about their experience of your presence—data points rather than judgements on what they saw, heard, and felt, plus any specific observations you asked for.

- To add to the experience, record the session and review it together as you get the feedback.

My 10-step presence ritual for getting ready to host in a virtual space

1. A final rehearsal and check connections—checking lighting, sound, and 'Zoom Zone' (what people will see behind me when I start my video).

2. Final chat with my co-host/technical host if I have one, to agree on how we will communicate during the session.

3. Set up a second screen: usually a laptop for back up and to see what attendees see. I also set up my iPad if I think some participants will be using one.

4. Clear all distractions: emails, phone, closing windows on my computer to free bandwidth.

5. Move away from the screen, sit in a comfy chair, feet on the floor and ground myself.

6. Breathing exercises with eyes shut to center myself: breathing deep into my belly, out for a longer count than breathing in if I am feeling anxious.

7. Set my intention for the session: using myself to support the group's work and provide a presence that may be missing in the system.

8. Stand in front of the computer and mentally open the space for people to enter.

9. Open the room 15 minutes before the start time and imagine everyone entering a room. Welcome everyone by name as they join, making eye contact, and slowing down my speaking speed.

10. Think: Connection before content.

Practical considerations for online presence

Some of us work from an office or home office space, and some of us may be working from the kitchen or a table somewhere else in our home. Here are some practical considerations for your online presence:

1. Raise your laptop, monitor or iPad to eye level so you can look straight into the camera (books or a stool will help). This improves your connection with the group and increases your impact.

2. Either sit or stand, depending on what is comfortable for you.

I prefer to stand as it replicates the energy I have when I'm facilitating in person. Have your head and shoulders visible on the screen; not too close as that can be overwhelming, and not too far away, as you'll look like you're not interested. Check how much space is visible between the top of your head and the edge of your computer screen, and adjust accordingly.

3. Try to have a natural light source so people can see your face, and don't sit with your back to a window, creating a mysterious shadowed figure. If you regularly host or work online, then a well-positioned desk lamp or investment in a halo light can help to replicate natural light. This enables you to adjust the lighting on your face so there is not too much shadow and soften harsh overhead lighting.

4. Consider what people see 'behind you', as they'll get a unique window into your life. Remove anything you wouldn't want them to see, or reposition your desk/table to create an on-screen working zone or 'Zoom zone' free from distractions. Some platforms have the option to be able to blur the background. Also, consider how to create an inclusive environment that doesn't display symbols of privilege that may be seen and experienced by others as excluding.

5. Minimize background noise by staying on mute unless you are speaking. If you can't be in a private space, wear headphones for better sound quality. Again, if you regularly host or work in a virtual space then a separate microphone is a good investment for improved voice tonality and quality.

6. You may want to use one of the many virtual backgrounds available, or to create your own so that your personal home space remains private. Consider investing in the rigging and cloth for a green screen, which you can purchase and assemble for a relatively small amount of money. That allows you to create any background you want without the annoying fading in and out of fake backgrounds that can happen without a green screen or high-specification computer.

Hosting Roles

There is a difference between hosting and facilitating in this context that is worth exploring.

Some definitions describe facilitating as a mechanistic approach to help a group solve a problem and move to a fixed end state, something that is done to a group in pursuit of a goal in a disassociated and neutral way. By contrast, hosting is described in a blog by Corrigan (2007) as "leading from within a living system . . . where there are no answers, but instead only choices to make around the next question, and the paths where those questions lead us."

I think this creates an unhelpful dichotomy, an either-or sense. Am I a facilitator or am I a host? I prefer to view it as a continuum. At one end, I may be more of a facilitator, actively guiding the group towards a goal or outcome, focusing on creating and following the agenda to achieve an outcome, facilitating conversations and capturing key points along the way to reach the desired endpoint. At the other end of the continuum, I am more of a host in the way I am creating an environment where people can work on their own. I'm present to what is emerging and unfolding, less fixed on a 'right' output or outcome, more creating the conditions where the group have ownership of how they are working and capturing their outputs. I'm supporting and encouraging them to work in the spirit of co-creation and collaboration, working with transparency about shared choice points to adjust what happens next and what I notice is happening. The reality is that I flex along that continuum depending on what is needed by the client, their situation, and the dominant organizational narrative.

As a Dialogic OD consultant, I follow the Generative Change model (Bushe, 2020), where the role of host is to bring people together in a useful and collegiate way, ensuring they have what they need (McKergow, 2020). I work to help frame purpose statements and engage stakeholders in generative conversations before supporting an iterative process of dialogue and experimentation.

Hosting is less active than facilitation in following a set agenda or nudging the conversations along. This doesn't mean that there isn't lots of planning done beforehand. The planning is essential but held lightly once a workshop starts. It's a sound starting point. Hosts provide the broad framework for generative conversations and dialogue, create a space where people feel safe and able to contribute freely without fear of recrimination, and then step back to see what is happening. When we are less involved in the content of what is being discussed, we can notice how the group is working as they begin to work and interact. We can pay attention to who is contributing and who is silent, if unexpected topics are emerging that need to be addressed and making dynamic adjustments in the moment depending on what emerges.

Some will say this description is of a skilful and experienced facilitator, on top of their craft, being able to be fully present, accessible, and flexible to respond to the situation. Whatever the label, at the core of being fully present, accessible and flexible is to have 'presence' and be able to use the best of yourself.

Working with a co-host and technical host

Depending on the kind of workshop or session you are hosting, you may want to consider extra support. Co-hosting is an excellent way of sharing the workload and bringing diverse skillsets to a workshop.

A two-hour workshop often needs at least two people. That could increase to three or four depending on the complexity of the design (breakout rooms, voting polls, capturing outputs, etc.) and the familiarity of the hosting team and participants in using the technology platform you are working on. Involving others in a hosting team can remove some stressful moments. Thoughtful planning, and rehearsing the workshop with your co-host ahead of time, will help you identify any tricky sections or transitions that need special attention.

Technology can sometimes be troublesome and, despite full preparation, we can be interrupted by technical issues. Creating contingency plans with your hosting team for computer failure or internet connectivity problems will relieve stress if that happens. A co-host taking over the 'controls' as host, logging on with an additional computer, having access to a back-up Zoom or Microsoft Teams account, and having access to an additional means to connect to the internet, can cover most technical problems.

These are four roles that need to be fulfilled, either by one person or across a hosting team:

1. **Host or Facilitator:** Holds the focus on content/task for a workshop or a session, briefs the group, and holds the container's boundaries. (This is not the same as the Zoom host).

   • Be real! Be a human on camera rather than trying to be perfect.

- Be clear with instructions and make invitations for people to speak using their name.

- Don't be concerned if you need to refer to notes or check with your colleagues on timings or technical aspects. We do all of these things when we facilitate workshops in person, so why not virtually too?

- Be grounded in your presence and how you show up

2. **Co-Host:** Reads the room, pays attention to group process, relational dynamics, tracks contributions and energy. Interrupts to draw attention to what's being said or not being said, intervenes to draw attention to dynamics to improve how the group is working.

   Captures outputs on pre-prepared templates, on whiteboards, in Chat by participants, or on slides 'live', or in the background (if the group or a note-taker isn't doing this).

   This role can also monitor Chat and feed themes back into the group. Alternatively, the group can be encouraged to do this themselves. Remember to save the Chat messages before the call ends if you want to keep comments or questions from the group.

   These first two roles will often rotate during the workshop, as you would do in a physical place.

3. **Technical Host (sometimes called Technical Producer):** Someone who is confident and skilled with using the virtual platform and technology. They run all the technical aspects, manage time, create breakout rooms, and prepare attendees before the event. They also oversee and brief on using any collaboration tools. This is what Zoom calls 'the host'.

   This role is also the trouble-shooter for any technical issues that might occur—internet access difficulties, technical problems, connecting a video feed with a phone in line, or re-admitting participants who may have dropped off the call. Because such issues arise unexpectedly, if you don't have a technical host it will be very difficult to continue facilitating the group's work while managing a participant's technical problems.

   Other than being introduced at the start of the call, the technical host can choose to turn their video off to focus on the technical tasks. It's helpful for them to add 'technical host' or 'Producer' to their name.

4. **Notetaker:** This is an optional role and depends on participants' confidence levels with the technology and approaches used for capturing outputs. If required, they can capture outputs on pre-prepared templates, on whiteboards, in Chat, Google Docs, or another app, or on slides 'live' or in the background if participants aren't doing this.

This role can also monitor Chat and feed themes back into the group.

Communicating as a hosting team

There are times when a hosting team needs to check with each other on how things are going and agree if dynamic adjustments are needed to the session plan. In virtual space it's trickier to quickly chat and adjust the session in the way you might do in person. Stepping to one side for a conversation becomes more difficult too. There are several ways you can communicate as a hosting team; the most important thing is to agree on how you will do this before the session starts.

- Via private Chat: Useful for occasional messages but only works if there is only one other person in the hosting team. Please take care to make sure your message isn't being broadcast to the whole group.

- WhatsApp: Setting up a WhatsApp group for the hosting team is a good way to have ongoing conversations during the workshop, but can be distracting if you are 'on stage'. It's a good idea to have an alternative messaging option to the internet in case one of you loses internet service.

- Breakout Room: Setting up a 'host' break out room is a great way to have a debrief during the workshop, either during a break or while the groups work in breakout rooms.

- An explicit agreement for a co-host to interject—this works well if it has been contracted for and the group is aware it may happen. Great when there is an agreement to work on group dynamics and share observations, and if you are being transparent about how you work and make dynamic adjustments when co-hosting.

> Example:
>
> For each workshop in a series run with an Executive Team there was a facilitation team. This was made up of Lead facilitator, Co-facilitator and Technical Host, who all collaborated to create the design. The team was supplemented on the workshop by two notetakers.
>
> In the initial workshops at the start of the program the Executive Team were supported by a facilitator and a notetaker in each breakout room they worked in. This was to guide them through some difficult conversations, allow the team members to focus on making contributions rather than being concerned about the technical aspects of capturing outputs, and for the newly-formed team to establish working norms.
>
> As the team matured and became more familiar with working virtually, they self-managed breakout sessions.

Creating Psychological Safety in Virtual Spaces

"Psychological safety exists when people feel their workplace is an environment where they can speak up, offer ideas, and ask questions without fear of being punished or embarrassed." (Edmondson, 2018, p.10). Professor William Kahn (1990) described psychological safety in his study on employee engagement as "feeling able to show and employ one's self without fear of negative consequences to self-image, status, or career. People felt safe in situations in which they trusted that they would not suffer for their personal engagement" (1990, p.708.). In essence, it is when you feel safe to be yourself and voice your opinions in your team or the group you are working in.

Taking steps to build psychological safety online enables us to create shared experiences and deeper relationships within a team or group. These bonding experiences release oxytocin into the bloodstream, promoting feelings of attachment and trust, and dampen cortisol (the stress hormone). Increased oxytocin boosts our mood and productivity and facilitates greater collaboration. Without psychological safety, our fight or flight response kicks in, closing down perspective and reasoning and reducing creativity and the willingness to cooperate with others. This is the opposite of what we want for our dialogic and generative work. When we feel safe, we become more open-minded, resilient, motivated, and persistent. Humor increases, as does our capacity for creativity and divergent thinking, idea generation and finding solutions (Delizonna, 2017).

Building psychological safety online:

We need to create a safe space online where people can contribute without feeling exposed, embarrassed, or marginalized. There are some factors to consider regarding the level of psychological safety required for your work. For example, a greater level of psychological safety needs to be created for personal development sessions compared to generative working sessions. You need to use different approaches to establish psychological safety with a large group of stakeholders who have never met compared to an intact team who already have agreed on norms and ways of working.

In some respects, in virtual space people can be more open as there is a kind of disassociation from reality that exists when we are not physically present with each other. In other respects, it can be easier to withdraw, be silent, and switch the camera off.

Below are some of the questions a Dialogic OD practitioner usually considers to estimate the extent to which psychological safety will need to be increased for the session to work well.

- Do the participants all know each other? How well do they know each other?

- Are they used to working together virtually and already have some agreed norms/ways of working that you can use?

- What's the normal way of doing business, and now that we are in a virtual space how does that change?

- What is the cultural impact of hierarchy and power in the system, or multiple systems, that might show up?

- What positional power will be present in the workshop, and is that likely to cause some people to feel intimidated?

- What likelihood is there for people to encounter risk or exposure in the workshop design?

- How much consideration of different points of view is needed in the workshop to reach the outcome?

While these questions aren't different from ones we would consider before running a workshop in a physical place, the approaches we use to create psychological safety in a virtual space need some adjustment. Psychological safety can be created at three different stages for an online workshop, and each of these build on the ones before:

1. **In the Design stage,** to identify the pivotal moments in the workshop where safety is required most and consider which approaches are best suited to do that. Because virtual sessions are shorter there is a need to start to build safety before a workshop as well as during a workshop. The design stage is where both are these are considered when working in virtual spaces.

2. **In the Preparation stage**, to gently use lower-intensity activities that create inclusion and build connection and trust. This stage becomes more critical during virtual spaces, and thoughtful preparation can enable deeper work to be done during the workshop itself.

3. **In the Active Participation stage.** This is where most of the work is done to build psychological safety by layering different approaches that deepen trust. If sufficient thought has gone into the design and preparation stages, then there is a good base for greater safety and trust to be quickly established here.

Table 4 looks at different considerations and approaches for psychological safety to be built at each of the three stages.

Table 4: Building Psychological Safety at Different Stages

Stage	Considerations/approaches for building psychological safety
Design	• Consider what could be done in the preparation stage to begin to build psychological safety • Create time at the start for each person to speak and share something about themselves • If the group or team regularly work together, help them get to know each other at a deeper level
Design (continued)	• If you are working with the same group over multiple sessions, design time in each session for deeper understanding and disclosure • Allow space in the session plan for participants to shape and add to what is explored/discussed • Working in pairs and small groups in breakout rooms builds safety and confidence to contribute • Use polls to check levels of agreement/shared views • Allow for screen breaks, incorporating physical movement to stretch, and 'walking paired work' that can take place by phone
Preparation	• Be clear about what people can expect when they attend • Be clear about confidentiality, what will happen to the outputs from the session, and the level of anonymity • Let people know if the session will be interactive and that it's important for them to be seen with their video on and to make contributions • If required, ask them to be in a private space without being disturbed • Ask people to think about what they need to create a safe and trusting environment and create a shared space to share those thoughts before the workshop • Offer short technology briefing sessions if you are using unfamiliar platforms and apps
Active Participation	• Greet people by name as they arrive, and refer to their names during the session where possible • Ask everyone to use Gallery View so they can all see each other. Ask everyone to keep their cameras on for the entire session unless there is a point in the design where something different is required.

Stage (continued)	Considerations/approaches for building psychological safety (continued)
Active Participation (continued)	• When everyone has arrived, share that fact, and invite everyone to take a moment to settle themselves, both feet on the floor, taking a few deep breaths and in silence. This helps people fully arrive and join the session, rather than being distracted with whatever they have just finished doing • If appropriate, slow the pace down by doing a short connection/breathing exercise or guided meditation to focus on the intent/purpose of the session • Invite everyone to look around their surroundings, feel themselves sitting in the chair, turn inwards noticing their inner space, and then finally scan the screen to take everyone in. Encourage them to look at everyone in turn, imagining eye contact. This creates a field of connection • Entering where people are located geographically, at home, in the office, helps people to locate themselves and each other • Once everyone has arrived, allow each person to get their voice heard with a check-in question (see the list below) and to contribute without being interrupted • Use paired or small group conversations to set their own ground rules about what is and isn't acceptable Eg: turning off self-view if it is distracting, when it is acceptable to switch your video off, mute or no mute, breaks, etc. • Confirm the need for confidentiality within the room, what will happen to contributions and outputs from the session, and the level of anonymity. If it is recorded, who the recording will be shared with and where it will be stored. • Be clear on your role as host, your style, and how you will 'hold the space' for them to do the work • Find out what the standard way of doing business is when working virtually and how that may impact the way the group works • Create a deeper level of connection by asking them to select an item from home that is important. Each person shares what it is and why it's important • If appropriate, confirm/contract for the way you may observe and intervene. For example, using Chat to share what you notice about how the group works/intervene/support, versus speaking out when you intervene. Or the use of 'Pin Video' to watch an individual regardless of how is talking

Stage (continued)	Considerations/approaches for building psychological safety (continued)
Active Participation (continued)	• Be prepared to be vulnerable first and disclose something about yourself, modelling the level of depth you are hoping for from others • Role model a calm presence, showing curiosity to understand what's behind someone's contribution

Example:

At a workshop I attended, the facilitator and technical facilitator built psychological safety in a really effective way. The technical facilitator confirmed how the workshop would be run, which bits would be captured and shared, who they would be shared with, and how best we could participate. The facilitator stayed on screen the whole time during the workshop, showing occasional slides for very short periods of time. Her voice was calm and gentle, and she made few physical movements.

She began by sharing something about herself with a revealing statement, and after a couple of introductory statements about the workshop she invited us to contribute through Chat—the invitation was a gentle 'what are you here for?' She then continued to reveal more about herself with greater levels of disclosure each time she spoke. Listening to her it was like she was peeling layers off an onion. At this stage there was no requirement for us to do anything other than listen in a space that was feeling increasingly safe as she was being increasingly vulnerable.

We were placed into breakout rooms in pairs for a short conversation in response to a question, reassured that we wouldn't be asked to share what we spoke about. We were asked to reveal much less of ourselves in that paired conversation than she did of herself, yet despite working with someone I didn't really know, I felt sufficiently safe to reveal more about myself than I would have done without the way she 'went first'.

She built psychological safety for me through her willingness to be vulnerable first, and through her calm voice and gentle presence.

Check-in questions to build psychological safety and connection

Check-in questions are an important way of connecting everyone at the start of your online workshop. They help people to be fully present rather than still thinking about what they have just finished doing or will be doing next. They start the process of building connection, trust, and intimacy, all of which are the gateways to high-quality dialogue. The intent is to allow each person to be heard and get their voice into the conversation, rather than open a general discussion on what someone has said.

Depending on how many people are on the call and the time you have available, here are a range of questions you may want to try. Some are more 'task' focused, and some focus at a more personal level, which might be more appropriate if a group/team is working together frequently. The further down the list you go, the more personal they become:

- Who are you and what's your role in the organization?
- What is most important for you to get from this call?
- What is the contribution you want to make today on this topic?
- What is going surprisingly well at work this week?
- What is happening that might distract you from being able to concentrate and fully contribute?
- Rate your energy levels or enthusiasm for today's session on a scale of 1-10 (1 being low)
- What has been occupying your time/mind today?
- What has made you smile in the last 24 hours/this week?
- Tell us something you are passionate about.
- Share something about your name: how you got it, what you like about it.
- What three words describe how you are feeling right now? (No need to explain them further).
- How is your inner world today?

Other check-in questions for teams that regularly work together include:

- Bring your favorite mug and tell the story of why it's your favorite.
- Share something about you that may surprise others.
- Tell us one thing you are proud of.
- Tell each other the kindest thing you have done this week.
- Show an important item from your home, and share why it's important.

Tip:

To provide some structure and build participation, you can select who starts the check-in and then ask them to choose who goes next. The next person then continues to choose until the whole group has checked in. This can also be done by throwing an imaginary ball around the group, speaking the person's name before you 'throw' the ball to them. Alternatively, you can ask people to speak when they are ready. That may add more pauses or result in people speaking over each other, but it encourages people to pay close attention to others in the group rather than passively waiting for their turn.

> Example:
>
> When running a weekly project team call I led the check-in for the first couple of weeks and then asked for volunteers from the team to lead it in subsequent weeks. As different members of the team took turns the range of check-in questions became more creative and engaging, and we deepened our relationships with each other. Attendees took this approach to their own team meetings and a new pattern of building connections and deepening relationship at the start of meetings started to be replicated across the business.

Closing participation with 'check-out' questions

Check-out questions are an important way of allowing people to close out their participation and end the workshop, reflect on the value they are taking from the session, consider their contributions, and move to action. Allow time at the end of a workshop to enable each person to speak, and as with the check-in, the intent is not to open up the conversation further.

Here are some suggestions, brief and more in-depth:

- What did you want to say but didn't have the chance to? (This is a good question to ask as a final round of reflection before moving to check-out).

- What three words describe how you are feeling now?

- What do you notice about how you have worked together today?

- What has been most valuable for you during this call?

- Rate your level of satisfaction with the call on a scale of 1-10 (1 being low).

- What are you appreciative of?

- How are you leaving this conversation?

- What are you taking away from this conversation?

- What have you been moved by in this conversation?

Summary of key points from this chapter

- Our presence as Dialogic OD consultants is a cornerstone of our work.

- We need to adjust our presence when working online and consider how we look, sound and fill our space with our presence and impact.

- The way we host and facilitate online workshops can create an environment where people can work together in the spirit of co-creation and collaboration.

- Planning the nature of our hosting is essential, as well as having the ability to step back once a workshop has started to see what is happening and make dynamic adjustments as they are needed.

- Working with a co-host and technical host enables us to be fully present to what is unfolding during a virtual workshop.

- Creating psychological safety happens through our design, how people prepare, and through the activities we use to create connection and inclusion.

- Check-in questions can build connection, relationships, and safety.

PART TWO

Mastering Virtual Consulting

SIX

Group Process

This chapter looks at the first two elements of group process consulting: noticing and tracking, and how we can adapt this method of Dialogic OD to working in a virtual space.

Group Process

One of the foundations of OD is the concept of *process consulting* (Schein, 1969). The consultant helps the client system better understand 'how' they get their work done instead of 'what' they are doing. To do that, we focus on helping the client perceive, understand, and act on several core relational processes. Schein identifies six of these:

1. Communication

2. Member roles and functions

3. Group problem solving and decision making

4. Group norms and growth

5. Leadership and authority

6. Intergroup cooperation and competition

Marshak (2020) has added a few more dialogically oriented processes to pay attention to:

7. Narratives, storylines and themes

8. Explicit metaphors, analogies and word images

9. Implicit metaphors

10. What is not said or deemphasized

These core group processes are equally relevant when we are working in a virtual space. What changes is the range of data sources we can draw from to notice, track, and intervene.

The flow of our work as dialogic consultants is to *notice* what is happening while a group is working, to follow the group's process (*tracking*), and to share what we've noticed with the group (*intervening*). We share what is helping and what may be hindering the progress of the work they are doing. Over time, we may encourage and support the group to notice and adjust their processes on their own, so they become self-reliant.

To notice and track in a virtual space we need to amplify our attention through deep listening (Marshak, 2020), tune into more subtle visual clues of body language and facial expression, and dial-up our embodied knowing that comes from sensations and feelings arising within our body. The field of somatics or "looking at oneself from the inside out" (Hanna, 1988, p.20) is important for process consulting, both in physical and virtual spaces. Developing the ability to tune into our somatic self; our internal awareness of feelings, movements and intentions, is a central element of embodied practice that OD practitioners need to cultivate.

When I work online, I notice that the physical configuration of sitting in front of a screen creates a disembodied sense. My head can easily feel disconnected from my body. If I'm not careful, I can prioritize logical, rational data and lose touch with the data my body can provide me; my somatic data. To notice and track group process effectively, I need to ground myself and become more aware of my body.

> Example:
>
> Before I host a virtual session, part of my preparation is to sit with my feet solidly on the ground, to feel my body in my chair, and to go through a breathing practice to ground myself into my body. I need to tune in more deeply with my whole self first before I can connect with others and the situation in front of me on the screen.

This practice of embodied sensing or "the capacity to experience others and the world around us ... through an attentive awareness of our body sensations, feelings and sensory information" (Chidiac, 2018, p. 61) is the way I do this. I pay close attention to the physical sensations, emotions, and feelings that arise within me, and combine those with what I hear, notice, and think. I cannot apply this attention to others until I have first tuned into my somatic self.

Working with a co-host to 'read the room'

It's challenging to scan and notice what's happening while presenting because you're trying to engage and connect through the camera. Working with a co-host in virtual spaces is essential if you want to attend to group process. While the host is presenting or briefing the group, the co-host is scanning the virtual room, observing people on the screen, or across multiple screens if it is a large group. Groups of between 12-15 are an ideal size for virtual process consulting, as everyone is visible on one screen and you can easily see their faces. Tracking large groups in a virtual space can be tricky, and if you are working with a larger group, then setting up more screens allows you to see the whole group. If you are using virtual process consulting in breakout groups, then each breakout room will need a host to support group process.

The co-host uses the gallery view and is listening intently, watching people's faces. There are fewer data points in virtual spaces, with fewer visual cues, so we rely more on listening to what is being said and how it's being said. Here are some of the adjustments needed for when we are noticing, tracking, and intervening in virtual workshops.

Noticing

When I'm in the co-host role, these are some of the things I pay attention to regarding body language and facial expressions in a virtual space. These observations center around the head, face, and upper torso, as that is often all we can see:

- I notice how people position and move their head: the tilting to one side may mean someone is listening hard and deeply engaged, dropping the chin, and looking down may mean someone is thinking.

- I look at people's eyes, noticing the eye movement pattern around the screen, or a widening or narrowing of the eyes that may indicate an unexpressed reaction to what's been said. I also check for signs that someone may be multitasking/reading emails and their impact on their contributions.

- I look at the mouth: how soft or firm is the mouth, how often someone smiles or laughs.

- I watch when people lean forward and move towards the screen, or sit back and move away—what was said that triggered the movement? Do they move forward when they want to speak? Do they move forward but not speak?

- I notice breathing patterns: when they take a deeper intake of breath than normal, or let out a long sigh.

- I notice how much people fidget or remain still and what triggers those responses.

- I notice whether an individual's movements and expressions are a one-off or repeated to form patterns.

I also notice the language used and the metaphors that emerge in the conversation. Who are the individuals who use these metaphors, and are they commonly held across the whole group or just some of the members? What other metaphors are spoken about? Do any different metaphors join up in some way?

I try to resist the temptation to interpret what I see. My interpretation may be right, but it may not. My first action is to notice and track to see if there is a pattern emerging or if what I'm noticing is connected to another person/other people's actions or inactions. I'm curious to know if some movements or expressions are expressed in words or if things are not being said.

Tracking

When I track, I'm looking for:

- Repeated occurrences of what I may have noticed that form a pattern.

- Patterns of contribution: who speaks the most, who initiates ideas, who supports or opposes them.

- Interpersonal dynamics: are there small groups of people who trigger patterns of behavior?

- Impact: who gets attention when they speak, where are the influential voices, and who gets ignored?
- The generative approaches used and how decisions get made. Is there an explicit process for making decisions?
- How does the group deal with disagreement? Is it smoothed over, surfaced for discussion, or do 'spiky' exchanges take place?

When I'm tracking during a virtual session, I pin the participants on the screen—this feature in Zoom stops peoples' video feeds from moving around the screen if they switch their camera off or we move into and out of breakout rooms. In some regards, the screen has become my circle, although not in a true sense as it is easier to see people when they are on the screen than sitting in a circle.

With features like 'Pinning' and 'Speaker View' on Zoom, we are closer to peoples' faces than we would be if we were sat in a circle co-located. Everyone can see everyone face-on. 'Speaker View' and 'Gallery View' allows us to see individuals close up, at the same time as seeing the whole.

Depending on the nature of the work and the size of the group, you may need to have more than one co-host tracking, although the nature of the process work you would undertake with a large group may be more light touch than working with a smaller intact team like an Executive Team.

Example:

When facilitating a group of 30 people with a co-host, I joined the workshop for a second time from a separate laptop using a separate zoom account. I switched the video and audio off so there was no sound interference in the meeting.

My co-host and I took turns tracking the group while they were working. I was able to do this by using both screens. We had contracted with the group to observe and share those observations with them either while they worked, or during a scheduled review point on the agenda. We had built in a review point after each break and prompted the group to do their own individual reflection during their break. Throughout the series of workshops, the group became more tuned in to their working process and adjusted with less prompting.

Tuning in

As you track the group on your screen, patterns will emerge over a short period of time, and some things will become more noticeable or figural; work with those. Pay full attention to how you feel when you are tuned into your embodied senses and stay connected to your whole body, not just your head and thoughts. Being focused and open to what is emerging in front of you keeps you connected and in the present. That 'felt sense' starts typically as a sensation then emerges into a hunch or a feeling. Stay open to that feeling, trust it, and tune into it when it occurs.

A colleague of mine talks about working with 'strong backs and soft fronts' (Scarrott, 2020) when she tunes into groups. This phrase comes from the teachings of the Buddhist Roshi Joan Halifax, where she speaks of the relationship between equanimity and compassion (Halifax, 2010). With a strong back (equanimity), we have a calm composure. We are able to be grounded and strong while remaining flexible, adaptable, and open to change. With a soft front (compassion), we can be open to things as they are and meet others with understanding and empathy.

Remember that participants will be experiencing emotions and feelings, although they may be less willing to acknowledge and express those; they may come with a hard back and a hard front. As we practice cultivating our own strong back and soft front, we have the potential to connect to the emotions of those present through their facial expressions, body movements, and body posture, and bring those to their awareness.

Over time you will develop a felt sense of the group. When we are working online, we have what Leema (2017) calls an 'embodied presence'. That is, we are in the present moment at the same time, and we create a collective embodied presence when we come together. She says, "... in cyberspace we are still embodied. What changes is the experience of our own and the other person's embodiment." (Leema, 2017. Pg 92). Just because we are not physically together we still have an embodied experience. Due to the nature of the way we connect through video and screens, we experience our connection and the connection of others differently, in ways that we may not notice as readily as when we are together physically. We have an embodied experience when we respond to what we see or hear through the screen; we laugh, we cry, and we can feel joy or frustration during our interactions and exchanges. Part of our work, when we use our OD process skills in a virtual workshop, is to encourage the group to notice what is happening for themselves and each other right now.

When we work in this way, we are ready to absorb and work with whatever emerges with an open heart, being of service to those transformative spaces and the human development that occurs in them.

The autocratic nature of Zoom

Before we move on to making interventions in virtual workshops, it's worth looking at how working online has adjusted some of the power dynamics that exist in organizations and how that impacts our dialogic work.

Working online flattens the organizational hierarchy in an instant. Suddenly everyone has the same amount of space on screen irrespective of their role or authority, with no more politics about who sits next to who in the meeting. There's also something that changes regarding physical proximity within a group setting. As a participant, if I have a powerful and forceful contributor sitting next to me, their physical presence may diminish my ability to feel like I can speak up, whatever our relationship is. On a screen, we are all the same size with equal space.

You might have a team with much more vocal members than others, where you have a noticeable power dynamic that can disrupt or disturb when everyone is in a room together. Power dynamics change in a virtual environment; people can become more confident and comfortable speaking up, and some may not. Paying attention and giving consideration to inclusive facilitation approaches so all voices are encouraged and able to be heard is important to counteract invisible power dynamics that may remain.

> Example:
> When working online with an Executive Team for the first time, one of the newer team members commented on how the virtual working format 'democratizes contribution'. He shared that as a new member of the team he felt able to say more when working online. He felt he was heard in a way that wasn't happening when they were physically together in a room. He also noticed that other newer members of the team were contributing more in this environment too.

As hosts, too, the distancing nature of working through a video screen can make it easier for us to be more courageous with what we say and how we say it. Speaking uncomfortable truths to those in positions of seniority or power may feel easier when symbols of power do not surround us in offices.

An implicit democracy is visually built into Zoom which creates an equal share of space and invites an equal share of voice. At the same time, it is autocratic with time boundaries. When a breakout room closes, it is closed irrespective of who may be speaking or what is being said. Everyone is suddenly pulled out of the room, sometimes mid-sentence, and put back into the main room with everyone else. The conversation ends whether you're ready for it to end or not. The little message that says you've got 60 seconds left is a real leveler and demands compliance and brevity.

The dominant narrative within an organization's culture may be too firmly held in place for hierarchical power dynamics to be equalized when working online. In the early stages of a dialogic assignment, it may be prudent to consider the hierarchical configuration of groups coming together and whether the culture is such that contributions may be hindered if hierarchical levels are mixed too much initially.

Example:

The first generative working sessions of a consulting assignment were configured to bring small groups of people together from similar hierarchy levels. This was done due to the strong cultural norms, where those holding positional power were seen as 'right'. At the early stages we didn't want that to hinder and restrict the contributions from more junior leaders who might hold different perspectives. These junior leaders were also less comfortable and unfamiliar with attending online workshops and meetings due to the operational nature of their roles, so we wanted to minimize the barriers to their full engagement.

SEVEN

Making Virtual Interventions

This chapter looks at the third element of group process consulting and how we can intervene in different ways during virtual workshops to improve the group's functioning. The final section of the chapter shares how our personal presence combines with the group's process to create transformative moments that matter.

Interventions

Intervening is described in an online dictionary as 'the act of becoming intentionally involved with a situation in order to improve it or prevent it from getting worse' (Cambridge Dictionary, 2020). In OD, the act of intervening is described as 'the making of observations, the introduction of learning experiences and other supportive procedures—designed or intended to affect the ongoing social processes.' (Nevis, 1997, p.48)

An OD intervention can be described as a big 'I' or small 'i' intervention (Tschudy, 2006. p.160). The big 'I' is a series of sequenced, planned, and structured activities intended to improve an organization's functioning (workshops, meetings, conferences). The small 'i' is how a consultant uses themselves and what they say to disrupt the status quo. This can range from feeding back observations of what has just happened, sharing a hypothesis, making a small comment or question that interrupts the flow of a conversation, to intentionally disrupting a pattern that a group is enacting.

It is the second description of intervention that I'm covering here, where the small 'i' intervention refers to "any comment, suggestion, or recommendation that the consultant makes to the group in the service of accomplishing the task" (Reddy, 1994, p.7). Interventions of this kind are made into the ongoing conversations, work, and dynamics of the group to improve what is currently happening. They are made at one or more levels of the system, individual, interpersonal, or group level.

Through a dialogic process consulting lens, interventions are the in-the-moment aspects of transforming talk (Marshak, 2020) that can help reframe potentially limiting mindsets and open up the possibility of more generative interactions.

Making interventions relies on the noticing and tracking we have done. At their best, they are swift and immediate, bringing attention to what is happening 'here and now'. There is an intuitive aspect to the choices we make in those moments; the choice to speak up and intervene, or to stay silent and continue to notice and track. Silence itself can be a powerful intervention.

The choices we each make will be influenced by our own 'use of self' (Jamieson and Davidson, 2019) and presence as a consultant, our personal range and being at ease with our approach of working in a virtual space, and how we flex it to respond to what is happening. These choices need to be aligned with what has been explicitly contracted for in our work. That will guide both the frequency and the intensity of what we draw to the group's attention.

Use of Self

As Dialogic OD consultants, the use of self is a cornerstone of our work. It is described as our 'practitioner DNA' where our presence is use of self with intent (Rainey Tolbert & Hanafin, 2006, p.72). In his classic text, *Organizational Consulting*, Nevis (1987) describes presence as the living embodiment of knowledge and the integration of knowledge and behaviour. This can also be described as how we turn up and what we do when we get there.

Being fully present and noticing what is happening, then responding to what is emerging, is a fundamental element of hosting in any environment. The use of ourselves to make dynamic adjustments to a session's flow (knowing when to extend a conversation at a certain point in a session rather than following the 'plan') and intervening to open up a dialogue or draw the attention of the group to notice its patterns and how it is functioning, are foundational aspects of using our presence and having an impact.

Making interventions in a virtual space

There are four ways I intervene in a virtual space: two involve me speaking directly to the group, and two are done via Chat. My co-host and I get permission to work in this way during our group contracting stage, either at the start of the workshop or during our first session together. *Table 5* describes each of the four ways to intervene, along with considerations for each approach.

Table 5: Ways to verbally intervene during virtual consulting

Way of intervening	Details	Considerations
Speaking directly to the group while they are working.	Interrupting the flow of dialogue and work to share simply and cleanly what I've noticed. I don't interpret what I've noticed; I offer it to the group as a neutral observation and invite them to make meaning of what I've noticed. This is the most common level of the system to intervene in this kind of setting, especially if this kind of work is new for a group.	Addressing my intervention to the whole group generates a lower level of intensity. A group may experience being interrupted as disruptive to their flow of conversation.
Speaking directly to one or more individuals while they are working.	I can address my intervention to an individual or a few people in front of the whole group.	This raises the intensity level and isn't something I would do in the early stages of working with a group as it may reduce the feeling of psychological safety and make participants hesitant to speak if they worry it will result in getting unwanted attention.
Speaking directly to the whole group during a reflective pause.	Using a planned or a quickly-created in-the-moment reflective pause, I may use this option to develop reflexive skills within a group and add my observations once they have shared theirs.	This is also an excellent way to slow the pace down and encourage all the group to notice what is/isn't happening. Those who have a preference for fast pace working can find it difficult to slow the pace down with reflective pauses.

Way of intervening (continued)	Details (continued)	Considerations (continued)
	I use Chat to track how a group is developing and functioning, highlight group dynamics, and develop group learning. I can use Chat to carry out a structured reflection and review point, slow the group down, and ask them to share what they are noticing through commenting in Chat.	I share in Chat what I've noticed while dialogue is taking place, which allows the group to choose to pay attention to my intervention, explore it, adjust, or carry on working. Group members can be distracted whilst reading Chat and participating in conversations.
Via Chat to everyone while the group is working.	As with the verbal interventions above, I can address my comment in Chat to the whole group or to an individual via private chat. My choice will depend on the nature of the work I am doing, the intensity level I want to work with, and the level of safety that exists.	
	This can be elaborated to create a continuous stream of observations that can be reviewed after a session to draw learning from.	This approach encourages and supports group learning and develops their reflexive process and adjustments to their working process.
	A different approach is for someone in the group to undertake the 'observing group process' role and be responsible for noticing, tracking, and intervening.	Intervening in Chat first can build confidence and create a record to review and learn from. If this is combined with recording a call, group learning can be amplified.
Via Chat to an individual.	I might interact with an individual through a private message to see what might be impacting their participation and check that everything is ok, or to acknowledge and celebrate their contributions.	This can help a participant feel 'seen' and valued, and could also create a sense of being 'watched' and 'judged'. There needs to be clear contracting.

Example:

While facilitating an Executive Team strategy session, there wasn't an explicit agreement to develop the team's effectiveness through process consulting. However, we did contract for pauses and points of reflection for the team as part of the planned approach. My co-host and I observed the group dynamics—noticing and tracking how the team went about doing their work and the team's relational dynamics. From my observations, I noticed a core group within the team who initiated most of the ideas; they supported each other's ideas and had a greater amount of air time. Newer team members contributed less and appeared to have fewer allies within the team. The team struggled to move from discussion to decision, with conversations recycling around a topic a number of times before a decision was made.

We asked them to share what they had noticed about how they worked together as a team. We then provided specific examples of what we had noticed, together with suggestions of what they could work on—getting contributions from all team members and co-creating a process for their decision making. That was a 'light' version of a reflective intervention to improve the functioning of the team.

Physical Interventions to shift energy

There are other interventions I might make in a virtual space that are more emergent and 'in the moment'. These are responding to what I notice about group energy, sometimes related to 'Zoom fatigue'. They involve physical movement and can shift energy or release 'stuckness'. They are simple and easily overlooked as essential interventions to improve the working process of a group. There are two basic ones; taking a break and physical movement.

You can see the energy dropping online by the expressions on people's faces, a level of disconnection with what's happening, and by the quality or frequency of contribution. Taking a short break and encouraging time away from the screen is a powerful intervention and can shift energy.

- Closing your eyes gives a release from the screen. Add a guided visualization, meditation, or play music as a soothing break.

- Working solo away from the screen, sitting comfortably or going for a walk, creating time to read or reflect on something as part of a session, then come back together to discuss it while it's fresh in mind.

Having space and time within the container of a session to think, absorb, and reflect allows the experience to soak and marinade; new perspectives and mindsets can emerge as a result.

To loosen up thinking or reframe a situation where the group is getting stuck, having everyone physically move at the same time can release stuck energy and shift thinking. It's easy to forget that people can move while in front of a screen, and physical movement is great for experimentation. It creates a different mental state and opens up and builds new neural pathways for learning, innovation, and creativity. For example, you can pair people up on the telephone, ask them to go for a walk outside (if possible) and talk about what they notice about how they are working together and what they want to amplify when they get back to their desk and the call.

Playfulness and laughter release endorphins that create bonds within a group. A colleague described a group who 'held hands' through the screen. This brought an instant rush of joy and laughter as people realized that what they saw was not what the other people saw, but just doing the experiment brought connection and intimacy into the session. Another variation is for everyone to use their hands to show how they are feeling right now

> Example:
>
> When a group was avoiding making a decision, the host got them to stand up and move away from their desks, adjust their camera so they could be seen, and then asked them to sway, moving their arms and bodies around while they shouted out all the things people do to avoid making a decision—the more extreme, the better. The energy shifted and became more playful and innovative, and once they settled back down, a decision emerged.

These dynamic adjustments in the moment help you to stay anchored in the present. They enable you to be more responsive, available, and flexible, rather than fixed to a schedule on a piece of paper or feeling frustrated with where you might like the group to be.

Intervening in Breakout Rooms

Working in smaller groups in breakout rooms help people feel safer. There's a clearly-defined container and space that no one else can eavesdrop on. People can be more open and vulnerable. Relationships are formed, trust is built, and the conversation and work done can be more profound than in the main room.

Breakout rooms present challenges for a host. In a physical place, we can position ourselves in a room and tune into multiple conversations. If we approach a group, they see and sense us as we approach. We can't do that with breakout rooms; we have to go into a breakout room to see what is going on. When you join a breakout room, there is no warning; you just show up on the screen and may disrupt the layout of everyone's images on the screen. Your appearance is an intervention in its own right, and it can disturb their patterns and disrupt their working flow. We need to be much more thoughtful about how we come alongside to support, guide and help a conversation happen if it is stalling.

We need to consider how we elegantly enter and exit a breakout room.

1. To maintain the trust of the group and psychological safety, we need to be explicit and create agreements at the start of the session about visiting and leaving breakout rooms. This agreement depends on our role; is it to monitor how they're getting on, is it to support their working process, or to be available to respond to any questions if they need help?

2. When initially working with a group who are unfamiliar with each other, or the topic, I would set the expectation that someone will visit the breakout room early in the session to check on progress and answer any questions. I would also let them know that on entering the breakout room I may remain silent for a few minutes as I absorb what's happening, and then speak if needed. They are able to ask me questions when I show up, or carry on working and ignore me.

3. I set the expectation that I will quietly exit the breakout room when I'm ready to move on, and disrupt them as little as possible.

4. If the nature of the work means that a group will need support at some point during that breakout session, it can be less disruptive to have a facilitator present during the whole session. They do not need to be an active presence contributing to the task being done. They could be present in a process consulting role or just as a silent observer.

5. Once in the breakout room, I would adopt one of the ways of intervening that are outlined in Table 5 above.

6. Sometimes the need to visit a group is more about our own need to know what is happening, to check that things are progressing how we want, and to be able to feel we are helping. It can be better to leave a group to get on with things, to struggle a bit, and to know they have help on hand if they need it.

Example:

During a session five breakout rooms were working on generating a range of ideas. In the briefing for the session, I let them know that I would join each breakout room for a short time while they were working to offer support and answer any questions they might have, and that I would leave in a way that didn't disrupt their workflow. I also said that if they needed me at any time, they could send a message to ask me to join them.

I let the groups work on their own for the first part of the session and then visited each one in turn. When I arrived in the breakout rooms, I entered but didn't intervene straight away. I sat for a few moments to tune into what was happening, noticing the relationship dynamics. Some groups stopped talking as soon as I appeared and started to check that what they were doing was correct. Some groups continued working, and I waited for a pause before I spoke to ask how I could best support them.

In subsequent breakout room sessions, I left them alone to get on with what they were doing, emphasizing they could ask for help if it was needed. When I was satisfied that the group no longer needed me, then I exited the room.

Once groups are familiar with working in breakout rooms, I often leave them entirely alone and let them know they can ask for support by using the request help button in Zoom, or by one of them coming into the main room to find me. That then leaves me and my co-hosts free to have a debrief conversation. This can be done in the main room, or by joining a facilitator breakout room. The meeting host needs to stay in the main room, and can join the facilitator breakout room on a separate computer.

Creating transformative moments that matter

Creating a container for transformative moments means creating a space for possibility—where new ideas can emerge, new relationships get forged, and new agreements get made. It is a space of potential.

Because of the dialogic nature of things being created through processes of social construction and emergence, we can never really be sure whether a container will turn into a transformative space. There is a hopefulness in the way we create and host these containers, an unexpressed potential that is exciting to Dialogic OD practitioners.

A transformative space has the power to transform the thinking and actions of individual leaders. In turn, they can transform the interactions they have with others—what they choose to talk about and/or the way they choose to have that interaction. They will impact, and in turn be impacted by, that exchange and continue to transform others in future cycles of conversations held in similar ways. Transformative moments can also emerge from transformations in relationships among some or all of the people in the session, allowing new connections, information and actions to lead to organizational change. Perhaps the most profound possibilities come from 'ritual-transformative space' (Bushe, 2010), where archetypal patterns and unconscious processes are altered in fundamental ways.

A series of factors increase the likelihood of transformative moments that matter being created for clients.

Creating an invitational frame

The purpose behind bringing people together is an important starting point. How the purpose is framed will impact the motivation of participants to become engaged in the topic and the opportunity to create change. The topic has to be something people really care about, and one in which they feel there is a genuine opportunity to come together to contribute to generating new possibilities.

Connection and relationships matter

When people come together, connect, build relationships, and engage in generative dialogue, there is the opportunity for magic to happen. Transformative moments are when we all experience, either in ourselves or in a group, that something has shifted. We can feel it in our bodies, and it can be facilitated, maybe even amplified, through the medium of a digital platform. We know when we experience it.

Theories of group development have a phase where the group really comes together, when they have passed through the earlier stages of awkwardness, learning what each of them brings, how to get the best from each other, how to solve tensions and differences, and how to be in tune to maximize everyone's contributions, and performance is optimized. This is the space where creativity, humor, innovation and transformation springs forth.

Will and grace

Transformative moments that matter can't be intentionally generated; they work on the principle of 'will and grace'. The possibility is presented in the meeting of preparation (will) and opportunity (grace), and that is in relation to both client and consultant holding the intention that the possibility may occur. Preparation of the kind described in the earlier chapters of this book can set the stage in virtual consulting, but you and your client have to be open to the moments when an opportunity presents itself in relation to the collective energy of the client system you are working in. Transformative moments occur when there is a shared optimal experience of relational connection, safety and trust, curiosity and willingness for exploration, and collaborative generation of things that don't yet exist.

In her paper on the liminal space of change, Denham-Vaughan (2010) refines the concept of liminal space as being where two change processes meet, "when behind you lies all that is known, you stand on the threshold of the unknown to which the process of change leads you. This place, space and/or moment in time is characterized by a willingness to let go of anything familiar, and an openness to what is emerging" (p.35).

Being on this threshold and stepping past it requires 1) a willingness to let go of behaviors and ways of working that are familiar, and 2) the courage and curiosity to explore and embrace things not fully known or understood. Working in this liminal space requires using 'will' to get to the threshold and 'grace' to be open to what may happen next.

When I translate this into my virtual dialogic consulting work, my 'will' becomes all I have learned and experienced; my skills of working with groups, my knowledge of group theory and personal development, my ability to design and host transformative spaces online. This is what gets me into the space for full contact, and what helps me support my clients to be there with me.

My 'grace' is where I let go and step into the unknown, step into flow and make full contact with my client, safe in the knowledge that this is where the magic of transformative moments happen. My willingness not to be an expert with the 'right answer' allows me to meet my client in their willingness to step into an unknown space with me in generative dialogue and exploration.

I can't produce transformative moments without both. If I focus too hard only on 'will', my work becomes transactional. I'm following the carefully planned agenda, but those magic transformative moments will elude me. Conversely, those magical transformative moments of 'grace' can't happen without the technical skill base of my practice.

'Flow' is another way to describe it: the psychology of optimal experience featured in the work of Mihaly Csikszentmihalyi (2008). Transformative moments are generated at any of these three levels, but then there is a transformative amplification when they are concurrent.

Host in flow

Group in flow

System in flow

There are things a host can do to be ready for the opportunity of 'grace' when consulting in virtual spaces:

Host in flow:

- Fully present, centered and grounded.

- Accessing all expertise to make dynamic adjustments in the moment in a virtual space—reading the room, knowledge of relational and group dynamics, able to use a range of interventions at different levels of the system and different intensity.

- Prepared a core design and agenda as a base to improvise from and respond to what emerges.

Group in flow:
Rarely happens without a host in flow, and the host supports the group so that:

- Individuals are prepared for active participation.
- Everyone is focused and fully present.
- The group intent and ways of working are generative, dialogic, purposeful.
- They can move to convergence and alignment.
- They are motivated and committed to experiments and taking action.

System in flow:
The host works along-side the client system to co-create:

- A high-level architecture of the transformation arc.
- Nudging and disrupting status quo with multiple interventions.
- Participatory / dialogic approaches to generate high engagement, informal system communication, a movement being generated in pockets of energy.
- The generation of new patterns of discourse.

Creating transformative moments that matter is beautifully summed up by a colleague.

> "To work in this space of flow, we need to access our compassion, grace and humility when we do and extend the same to others. We cannot completely control the virtual spaces we create, just like we can't control those spaces in a physical place. Our work as a virtual Dialogic OD consultant starts with ourselves. It is what informs our practice now and for the foreseeable future. This state of life-long learning, knowing, doing, being, intentionality and choice in this virtual space." (Scarrott, 2020)

Summary of key points from this chapter

- Our work as OD process consultants is to notice, track, and intervene to improve the group's effectiveness. We can best do this when we work with a co-host.

- Intervening in virtual workshops can be done either by speaking to the group while working or through Chat. Intervening can happen in the main workshop room, in breakout rooms or privately.

- We need to consider how to enter and leave a breakout room elegantly.

- Transformative moments that matter occur when 'will' (the planning and technical skills of my practice) meet 'grace' (the way I respond to what is happening around me).

- These can't be planned; they emerge in the flow where preparation meets opportunity both for me a consultant, and for my client.

EIGHT

Whole System Spaces

In this chapter, I look at how to adapt some of the common dialogic large group approaches for virtual spaces. This chapter assumes that the reader is familiar with these different Dialogic OD methods. If not, a quick Google search provides links to full descriptions. You can also download the free, well-curated bibliography of 'Tools and Methods of Dialogic OD' by registering at the B-M-Institute.com website.

The very nature of bringing representatives of a whole system into a room together implies that a larger than standard group of people are coming together for a purpose. It may be to inquire into something of significance for that system, generate many pilot projects, produce proposals or agree on the way forward. In a physical place, these would typically be at least a one-day system gathering, or in some cases, two or more days of a single or integrated large group intervention.

A number of these dialogic approaches have been adapted for working either directly on Zoom or one of the other meeting platforms, or using add-on apps. These are some of the ways they can be successfully adapted.

Open Space Technology

There are three different ways to create an Open Space type conversation on Zoom. The first two are 'hacks' around the Zoom system, and the third depends on the version of Zoom the attendees are using. Unless you can guarantee all attendees are on a post-October-2020 version, it is a lower risk to use either of the first two approaches.

To create the opening marketplace of topics for an Open Space, you can use a collaboration tool like Mural to co-create the agenda and identify topics and hosts.

Approach 1

Once you have a list of all of the topics to be discussed, create the appropriate number of breakout rooms, and rename them by topic and/or room number.

- Ask people to identify the topic or room number they want to attend through the Chat. You will then manually send them to those rooms. This works for small/medium-sized groups, but for larger groups it is easier to ask people to rename themselves and put the breakout room number in front of their name e.g. '3 Gwen' means that I want to join breakout room 3, or 'Engagement Gwen' means that I want to join the group discussing Engagement. The technical host/producer then allocates everyone to the room of choice through the 'assign manually' option on the breakout room menu.

- When people want to move to a different breakout room they return to the main room and ask to be moved to the next room topic/number. You will need to have produced a list of the topics in each room that people can access.

- This approach's drawback is that it can be intensive for the technical host, can feel controlled, and the sense of freedom to 'butterfly and bumblebee' is reduced.

Approach 2

As participants join the meeting, or right before the Open Space session starts, make each person a 'co-host'. This gives them the ability to move themselves from room to room. It also gives them the ability to do several other things you may not want them to do, so you want to ask them to take care as they navigate around Zoom.

As previously, once you have a list of all of the topics to be discussed, create the appropriate number of breakout rooms, and rename them by topic. In addition, create an extra breakout room called 'Lobby' or some such name. Before co-hosts can move between rooms, they have to be sent to a breakout room by the host, so you will send everyone to this room first, and they can move themselves from there. It's a good idea to have a couple of spare rooms that might be 'Chill Out' or 'Coffee Shop' where people can gather for informal and emergent conversations.

- Move everyone into 'Lobby' and then ask them to select the conversation topic they want to join. Participants then go and join the room they want to visit.
- Once there, they can stay as long as they wish to, or move around from room to room to 'cross-pollinate' in Open Space style.
- The 'Chill Out' and 'Coffee Shop' are available for those who want to have some time to reflect or see who turns up for some emergent conversations.

Approach 3

This approach requires all participants to have Zoom software version 5.0 or later. Once the list of topics is agreed, and the breakout rooms are named, the host needs to select 'Let Participants Choose Room' from the breakout room menu. Participants then have full freedom to join the conversation they want and to move themselves from room to room.

With this option, I also include a 'Chill Out' room, where people can have a space to relax or for parallel conversations to emerge.

Other considerations for Virtual Open Space

Entering and exiting breakout rooms

I prompt a conversation to create shared expectations about moving between breakout rooms, how to enter and exit in the least disruptive way, and acknowledge that some people will come and go and not to take offence.

Design Harvesting Templates:

Create a simple template to capture conversation outputs and harvest in a consistent way. These can be prepared as individual documents or sections on a collaborative board that can be accessed as needed.

World Café/Knowledge Café

A World Café style approach can be replicated by using breakout rooms with a café host who stays in the room through three rounds of conversation as others come and go.

The café host shares the question or topic, guides thinking and creates a capture document that creatively summarizes the conversation themes as the conversations deepen. The themes can either be captured on a shared document or a collaborative Mural board so that the host can share them at the start of the next round.

The conversation groups are formed each round by the technical host either manually creating a different breakout group each time, or by allowing participants to select their own journey around each café room by making them co-hosts for each of the three rounds or using Zoom's 'let participants choose' function.

The final session takes place as one large group for collective meaning-making. The whole system 'gallery walk' can be nicely duplicated on a Mural board that the whole group can see simultaneously, concluded with a final round of reflections and actions.

This approach doesn't replicate the energy that's generated in a large room with the babble of multiple conversations occurring, and the 'café-style' environment that can be created with tablecloths, flowers, and pens. However, the nature of a fluid and developing dialogue within an overarching, generative topic can be maintained, and the table doodling can be captured on a shared Mural board for all to see.

Appreciative Inquiry

Working through the 4-D cycle of Appreciative Inquiry on a virtual platform like Zoom requires some careful thought. Here are some different approaches:

- Each of the Ds could be run as standalone sessions spread over several days. A collaboration platform can be used to capture the emerging conversations and be a visual record of the inquiry.

- The Discovery stage can be partly run using an asynchronous platform to conduct and capture the paired discovery conversations in the lead up to the first of the live sessions. These are then reviewed by the attendees before the first of the live sessions and developed into the first live session's positive core

- The Dream stage can follow at the same session. Working virtually presents the opportunity for much more creativity. Participants can use anything they can get their hands on in their own homes to co-create a representation of their dream of 'what will be'. Capturing these on a shared platform, with photographs, or by video allows for an easy way to share the dreams and develop emerging themes to position the Design stage.

- The Design stage can be a good time to work asynchronously again, with smaller teams working within an agreed time boundary to develop and share their work. Using a shared collaborative platform like Mural enables the whole group to see what's emerging and contribute.

- The final Delivery stage can bring the whole group back to a live event in the future.

A Digital Fishbowl

The fishbowl technique enables large group dialogue to take place on a topic in a dynamic way. It can help groups to develop a multi-faceted understanding of a complex issue, and get different realities in a room to reach new shared perspectives.

In a physical workshop, the fishbowl has an inner circle of chairs from which people speak, with one empty chair, while the remaining chairs form an outer circle. Those in the outer circle don't speak; they just listen. If they want to speak, they move into the inner circle and sit on the empty chair. They either step out when they are done, or they can stay and someone else in the fishbowl steps out.

This technique is easily adapted into virtual space on Zoom with everyone on Gallery View. Those in the 'inner circle' leave their video on, and those who aren't turn their video and microphones off.

To only see those in the 'inner circle', you ask participants to click on the three dots in the top right-hand corner of any participant box with their video off and click 'Hide Non-Video Participants'. The screen will then only show the participants in the 'inner circle' having the fishbowl dialogue.

When someone else turns their video on, they indicate they would like to sit in the empty chair and step into the dialogue by joining the inner circle. When they have finished their contribution, they switch their video off, leaving the empty chair for someone else to step into.

> **Example**
> In the first week of the covid-19 pandemic, a large department that provided necessary services to the entire department, and was geographically dispersed, used a digital fishbowl to engage the entire organization in emergency planning to decide how to continue to provide service while maintaining safe working environments.
>
> The five member leadership team fish-bowled their conversation and all 170 members of the department were invited to observe and participate through two open chairs, facilitated by a Dialogic OD consultant. Many difficult issues were surfaced including which functions could be done from home and which could not, how to reorganize onsite facilities to ensure safety, and concerns about fairness and equity. The explicit intention was that people's point of view would be heard and considered but that final decisions would be made by the leadership team. After two hours a plan emerged that had the understanding and support of most members of the department and was quickly executed, allowing the department to rapidly adapt with full alignment across geographical and functional boundaries.
>
> People commented that using virtual space created such an efficient and effective process it could probably not have been replicated in a physical place.

Just like me

Turning one's video on and off can be used to deepen connection by seeing who is 'just like me' and who's different. You leave your video on if your answer to the question is 'yes, that's me', or switch it off if it's not like you.

Once you see who has their camera switched on 'like you', there is an invitation for a moment of silent acknowledgment to notice who is there with you and how it feels to be seen and acknowledged by others 'just like me'.

It's an excellent way to know how diverse or similar the group is, create a greater sense of belonging and inclusion, and then work with what is revealed. Questions can be crafted to invite increasing levels of disclosure, with no pressure to participate. At the end of the questions, a group or team will have a deeper level of appreciation and understanding of each other.

NINE

A Virtual Dialogic OD Assignment

This chapter takes you behind the scenes on a consulting assignment where the approaches and ideas introduced in the book are put into action over eight months. I look at building a relationship with a brand-new client that I never physically meet, the different design choice points I faced, and what informed the choices I made. In the final pages of the chapter I reflect on what emerged that was unexpected, and consider what I would have done differently.

Background to the consulting assignment

The client was the Group HR Director for five specialist businesses operating under a Group structure with c12,500 employees. The operating environment of their business is specialist and technical, and they operate across multiple production sites. Despite the impact of COVID-19 on their operations, they decided to continue with a planned transformation program. As a result, all the transformation work was delivered through virtual working. The group of businesses were not used to working on virtual platforms.

The assignment's scope was to create a group-wide leadership framework to clarify what kind of leadership is expected now and in the future. This framework was to create a consistent experience of leadership across all businesses, and was the first collaborative project to be undertaken across the Group.

My role was to work with a small internal team (see Lewis, 2020 for an in-depth look at working with internal planning teams) and fulfil a variety of roles: to be the design architect of a co-creative process to generate the leadership framework, to guide them through the co-creation process, to work in partnership with the internal project lead, to be the lead host on some of the key workshops, and to build internal capability for this kind of work in the future.

This client was inexperienced and unsophisticated in their approach to virtual working—Level 1 on the organizational maturity framework shared in Chapter 3. Before the pandemic, they used telephone conference calls, some with video, which supplemented face-to-face meetings. The dominant organizational culture and narrative expected top-down leadership with a prescriptive and directive approach that followed expert inputs and used a diagnostic-based consulting approach.

Stages of the project

The different stages of the project map across the four processes of collaborative co-inquiry that are referenced in the BMI Dialogic OD Companion (Bushe & Marshak, 2020) you can download for free by registering at www.B-M-Institute.com.

Table 6 shows how each project stage maps against the four processes of collaborative co-inquiry.

Table 6: Project stages/collaborative co-inquiry process

Project Stage	Collaborative Co-Inquiry Process
Scoping + Contracting	Co-Missioning
High Level Program Arc	Co-Design
Co-Creation Workshops	Co-Reflection
Harvesting Working Sessions	Co-Reflection
Socialisation	Co-Action
Executive Endorsement + Sign Off	Co-Action
Roadmap for Adoption + Integration	Co-Action

One of the desired shifts in leadership behavior expressed by senior leaders at the start of this work, and by employees involved in the co-creation process, was to move away from hierarchical 'top-down' styles of leadership towards a blend of 'bottom-up/top-down', thus creating space for greater engagement and ownership at all levels. They wanted leaders to be less directive with a pre-determined solution and become more exploratory; encouraging a range of possible solutions to be generated and considered.

Some of the intentional principles within the design of this project were:

- the intent to widen the range of participation to include less commonly heard voices from across the system;
- to ask for volunteers as well as nominations;
- to use formal and informal networks to invite people to get involved;
- to seek out participation from different age, role, and geographic demographics;
- and to engage different specialist groups.

This approach was different from any taken previously and had the effect of disrupting previous patterns of the way projects and new initiatives were created and launched—a shift from 'done to' to 'working with'. The design of a series of discovery workshops and working sessions underpinned and influenced the generation of new narratives and discourses.

Micro-disruptions and participatory approaches

An early micro-disruption was to use the culturally different communication approach taken by the CEO, adopting his new weekly update video launched during COVID-19 to inform and engage the entire workforce. He created a specific launch video to announce the start of the leadership framework project, asking for volunteers to get involved and encouraging people who were invited to accept that invitation. The video triggered a positive reaction. People actively stepped forward and offered their participation. Every person who came forward was involved, every nomination was accepted, nobody was excluded from the process if they wanted to be involved.

An unexpected surprise for the project team and senior leaders was the positive energy and enthusiasm for improving leadership within each of the businesses. People were passionate about voicing their need for leadership to be different and willing to get involved. That hadn't been seen or heard previously to the same extent. The participatory approach tapped into previously unharnessed pockets of energy across the system, so much so that additional co-creation workshops were arranged, and a larger than anticipated project team was created to work with the outputs. Through the approaches taken on this project, and others within the broader transformation program, a new narrative started to be woven. New meanings were being created across the business through the interpretation of these new approaches, and it encouraged a growing discourse on the topic of leadership.

The unforeseen disruption of COVID 19 generated the need for new approaches to leadership and ways of working. In some respects, there couldn't have been a better time to lead in new ways when the foundation stone of traditional approaches had been cracked forever. Leaders were being asked to lead in a way they hadn't before, there was no script, and new role models emerged and thrived during the uncertainty.

Building client relationships in a virtual world

Before March 2020, most of my work was carried out by being physically present in client offices. My approach to building client relationships in this context was honed over many years. It has been more straightforward to shift existing client relationships into virtual spaces—I have a relational history, and relationship capital already exists. The shift for existing relationships is more about agreeing on the best way to work in a virtual space to deliver my services.

For new clients, I have continued to take a relational approach to my work. By this I mean blending a focus on *task* (what we are here to get done, discuss, or agree) with a focus on *relationship* (how we work together and co-create the nature of our emerging relationship and ways of working). My relational approach naturally invites dialogue: leading with my curiosity to learn more about my client's professional and personal world and how that shapes the work I am there to do; sharing what I'm noticing about the way we are interacting with each other, and reading cues that guide me as to when to probe more, or when to pause and shift focus. I anticipated doing this virtually would be more challenging.

Informal spaces

The informal spaces that contribute to building a new relationship—the time before a meeting starts, when we walk to a meeting room together, or the social chit-chat over a hot drink before the meeting begins—disappear in the virtual space. These need to be more consciously planned as it's too easy to dive straight into the content of a meeting when the 'Zoom clock' seems to tick more loudly. I found ways to create informal space at the start of a meeting, during a mid-meeting break, or at the end of a meeting.

Some approaches I used:

- We (my client and I) spent time at the start of our initial virtual meetings building our relationship. I was curious to learn more about what else was happening in her working world. This knowledge gave me insights into the 'task-related' part of our conversations.

- During our calls, I shared insight into my world, disclosing personal things and revealing insights into what else was happening in my working life.

- I happily opened up conversations about what could be seen in my home background behind me and used this to be curious about what I could see behind my client.

My client guided me as to how much time to spend informally; the conversation naturally shifted into 'task' mode when she was ready to start.

Formal spaces

As our conversation shifted, my primary focus was to continue building our relationship and deepen my understanding of her organizational context and the scope of what I was being asked to do. I used a blend of media—a mix of phone calls, Zoom calls, emails, and WhatsApp (later in our time working together). These all served to deepen my understanding, play back what I'd been hearing, share my experiences, confidently share my initial thoughts, build trust, be vulnerable, and hold a space for my client to be vulnerable and voice their concerns and anxieties.

These took place during a series of conversations rather than in a single meeting, and there were more conversations spread over a longer time period than there would have been face-to-face. In addition, there was more off-line preparation in order to be focused in the short time we were together. This meant anticipating more, being generous with my time and iterations during scoping and contracting, being reliable in delivering what I promised, and adjusting timing and pace to match my client's.

Technology

Through our conversations and my initial experiences of the organization, it became clear that there was a low level of technological maturity with working online (Level 1 in *Figure 6*). This knowledge was important in helping me shape the scoping and design options for virtual working. In this case, we used Zoom without any additional external applications as it wasn't possible for everyone to access those. If there had been a preferred platform, it would have been important to ensure that it gave the flexibility required for the designs and approaches I used.

We agreed on how we would store and share documents—that was ring-fenced within a secure system. Surfacing the technological freedom/restrictions early on helped me shape what was possible versus the ideal.

Personal and Purposeful

Reflecting at the end of the consulting assignment, my client identified these approaches as underpinning how we (my client and I) built our virtual working relationship:

- Personal and professional trust was built in parallel—it takes longer to build connections and relationships virtually, so we made time for conversations to explore and learn more about each other and our working/consulting philosophies.

- There were more frequent, shorter conversations than in past face-to-face consultations. We focused on our personal relationship first, making genuine human connections to build a deeper understanding. I found these shorter conversations more focused and productive than how we might have spent a whole day in face-to-face meetings.

- The dialogue that took place online was high quality. We wanted to ensure people felt heard and understood through accurate summaries and probing inquiry to discover more— our context was complex and nuanced.

- We wanted to feel safe enough to be vulnerable and share what was difficult in our work, feeling supported and not alone.

- Sharing information for discussion before our online sessions and working collaboratively during the session to co-create the next iteration. This purposeful way of working built professional trust, created clarity, and generated shared ownership in our collaborative partnership.

- Agreeing that all key communication would happen via one platform, so there was one place where everything was located to prevent confusion.

How the Design Unfolded

To co-create a new leadership framework the program arc emerged as a flow of connected interventions over eight months. This sequence of interventions was supported by a back-room 'infrastructure and transformation program office'. Cheung-Judge and Holbeche talk about the need for "back room change matters and front room change matters". The front room is the flow of interventions on the program arc—the "people dimension and the engagement" that the back-room infrastructure is supporting (Cheung-Judge and Holbeche, 2015. p.163).

The program arc was created against the backdrop of everyone working from home at the start of the program apart from essential on-site teams. There were high levels of anxiety and uncertainty amongst all employees during this time. Leaders were being asked to quickly adapt their leadership style and lead without knowing what would happen next. This business operating context set the frame for a series of conversations about leadership; what characteristics were needed for the future, and what was needed during times of uncertainty and ambiguity where no 'right' answer existed.

Figure 7 gives a representation of the Leadership Framework's program arc, where each of the four design approaches was used to create different containers during the eight-month project.

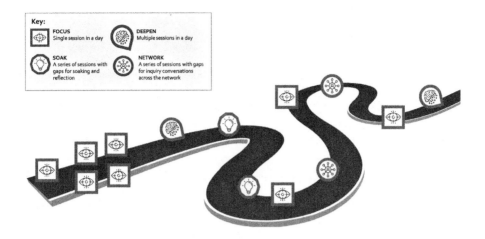

Figure 7: Leadership Framework program arc

Design choices

Each stage of this program had a different set of design considerations that influenced the final choice of the design approach used. These included:

- The purpose and outcomes of the workshop
- Where the workshop was positioned in the overall program arc
- Who would be attending
- The number of times the workshop would be run
- The workshop hosting team
- The complexity of what needed to be covered during the session
- The participants' level of confidence and experience using digital platforms

From these considerations, we mapped the workshops into one of the four design approaches, as shown in Table 7:

Table 7: Leadership framework design approaches

Workshop	Design Approach	Purpose	Participants
Co-Creation Workshops	**Focus** A single session lasting 120 minutes. Run multiple times.	For mixed groups of stakeholders to generate ideas for the next stage of developing the leadership framework.	Small groups of 12-15 people, multi-disciplinary, similar hierarchical levels. In total 600+ people to attend from across five businesses.
Group Executive Strategy Workshops 1&2	**Soak** Two sessions designed for the Executive Team, each lasting 150-minutes. A four-week gap in between for individual reflection and development of ideas.	To develop an HR strategy using inputs from preparatory discovery conversations and recommendations from a working group. To create a shared narrative and collective leadership approach to bring the strategy to life.	Group Executive Team of 12 people.

Workshop (continued)	Design Approach (continued)	Purpose (continued)	Participants (continued)
Harvesting Working Session	**Network** Three 120-minute sessions delivered over 14 days. Experiments and inquiry conversations took place across the network with key stakeholders between each session.	To harvest the themes and outputs from the Co-creation Workshops and create an initial draft of the leadership framework. Five small sub-teams created an inquiry and testing process across their networks before refining and creating a final draft.	A highly engaged small 'harvesting' team of 15 people with representatives from each business who want to continue to shape the leadership framework. This team worked in small sub-teams and as a whole team.
Executive Leadership Summit	**Deepen** Six sessions delivered in one day, each session lasting 45-minutes	To visibly endorse the leadership framework through this symbolic event. To co-create a shared narrative and alignment for co-action.	The Executive Leadership teams from all five businesses, plus the Group Executive Team. 60 attendees Team coaches for each of the executive teams.

Engaging with front line leaders

During the Co-Creation Workshops, there was a clear intent to involve a wide range of leaders from across all businesses. Many front-line team leaders worked in production areas with limited access to computers and the internet, so they were harder to reach and engage than others. These were critical voices to get involved in the early workshops as this was where the majority of leadership activity happened. Our program team used their informal networks and relationships to approach these leaders and engage them directly rather than through formal channels. We spent time getting to know more about their working shift patterns, identified suitable time windows to schedule workshops, and provided them with alternative ways to access the workshops and contribute via mobile phones.

Frame of Participation: Preparation

The Frame of Participation for each of these workshops required a different preparation phase, as shown in Table 8:

Table 8: Leadership framework preparation phases

Workshop	Preparation Phase
Group Executive Strategy Workshops 1&2	**Workshop 1** 1. Video from external experts sharing their perspectives on HR strategy development in this sector. 2. Slides outlining the purpose of the workshop and the output needed, a data pack summary of themes from previously held discovery conversations, and questions for individual meaning-making. 3. Individual pre-workshop technical familiarisation sessions to build confidence and comfort with using Zoom. **Workshop 2** 1. Videos from team members in each of the Executive's teams. A senior leader from within each Executive's team formed a working group who continued to develop the HR strategy between the first and second workshop. On the video, they shared key messages they believed were necessary for the Exec to hear regarding the draft HR strategy. 2. Each Working Group member briefed their Exec Team member and talked them through the draft strategy before Workshop 2. 3. A briefing document with the draft HR strategy.

Workshop (continued)	Preparation Phase (continued)

Co-Creation Workshops	1. Launch video by CEO
	2. Introductory email from facilitators, with an invitation for informal conversations to respond to questions.
	3. Slide pack:
	  a. outlining the purpose of the work.
	  b. sharing the framework to be used during the workshop.
	  c. questions to consider.
	  d. individual preparation to bring to the workshop.
	4. Pre-workshop technical familiarisation session.

Harvesting Working Sessions	1. Overview of the harvesting plan. 2. Briefing pack for Session 1. 3. Summary of harvesting work and test experiments for Session 2.
Executive Leadership Summit	1.Videos • Video 1 - The Group CEO and the summit host set the context and ambition for the event, setting expectations about the timeline leading up to the summit and preparation required. • Video 2 - Featured leaders from each business who had been involved in co-creating the leadership framework. They shared their reflections on their positive experiences of collaborative working during the co-creation process, the importance of leadership for them, and their hopes for a new leadership culture within their business. • Video 3 - from each Summit Team Coach briefing the executive team they were hosting on the preparation work they needed to do and offering support if needed. 2. Summit Workbook + Goody Bag • A printed workbook was sent to their home to guide them through summit sessions. This contained the preparation work, briefings for each session, spaces for reflection, and post-summit reminders. • Goody Bag: A collection of numbered packages sent to the participant's home and opened at key stages during the summit. The contents were designed to create curiosity, to act as a spark for idea generation, prompt reflection, and also provided food snacks to maintain energy.

Workshop (continued)	Preparation Phase (continued)
Executive Leadership Summit (continued)	3. Individual Reflection • This was a critical preparation activity, asking each participant to review their personal leadership style against the new framework, the outputs of which formed the content for the initial Senior Leadership Summit session. 4. Technical preparation • A short session at each Executive Team meeting before the event to share the features we would be using and answer any question they may have

Active participation in each workshop was generated by adopting the principles and approaches shared in this book's earlier chapters.

Hosting

Except for the Executive Leadership Summit, which is covered in more detail later, each workshop had a hosting team of at least three people; a main host, a co-host, and a technical host. Depending on the workshop's complexity, the participants' technical confidence, and participants' seniority, some workshops had additional support. These were mainly note-takers to capture outputs rather than having participants be concerned with this and distracting them from contributing.

Building internal capability

Internal hosts delivered the majority of the Co-Creation Workshops across the five businesses. I hosted some of the initial Co-Creation Workshops while the internal team built their skills and confidence. The hosts were volunteers from different departments in each business, not from the HR or L+D team. That was intentional and important; we wanted the work seen as a business-wide initiative rather than led by the Group HR function. Several briefing sessions and practice sessions helped these internal hosts build their skills and confidence.

Small internal teams of Zoom Magicians (ZM's) were trained to run each session's technical aspects. Many of the 600+ people involved were using Zoom for the first time, so alongside doing the work itself was a conscious process of gradually introducing more enhanced ways of using this platform. The ZM's often acted as scribes to capture the conversations and outputs, thus allowing internal facilitators and participants to focus on contributing to the exploration rather than being fearful of the technical aspects.

Executive Leadership Summit

The Executive Leadership Summit was different. This was a significant event and the first time the executive leaders from the five businesses had come together in this way. That in itself was a symbol of change, along with the collaborative nature of the project itself that involved people from all businesses working together for the first time.

The summit's overall purpose was to secure visible endorsement and sponsorship for the new leadership framework from each of the executive teams. This included:

- A shared narrative with which to describe the expectations of leaders.
- Agreement on how each executive leader and team will role model new behaviors.
- Generate ways in which the leadership framework can be fully adopted and come to life within each business and across the group.

Creating containers to build connection and safety

At the summit, our design needed to create a degree of connection and safety between a large number of participants in a relatively short space of time. Five intact teams were attending; many of the participants didn't know each other, while some had a history of working together. They were inexperienced at using digital platforms, and we needed them to work collaboratively and generatively.

The check-in and connection process at the start of the event was important. We wanted to build connection, give each person time to speak and be listened to, allow the speaker to reveal something about themselves, start to build safety, and allow participants to experiment with Zoom features. With 60 people joining, we made good use of the 'waiting room', admitting people as they arrived in small batches to welcome them, give them a brief technical tour, and quickly move them into small breakout groups of 3 or 4 people before the next group was admitted. These small breakout groups mixed people from different businesses; they had 10 minutes to introduce themselves and share something they were proud of having achieved recently.

Participants were then reconfigured into new groups, with people from different businesses, to continue to build connection and safety across the group; this time, they were invited to share a story of when a leader had a significant impact on them. The whole group came back together and were asked to share in Chat any themes, similarities, and differences they had noticed in their conversations. This check-in process set the tone for discovery through small group conversation, created new relationships between businesses, built an intimacy through being visible on screen, and contributing from their own safe space at home or in the office.

Main + Parallel Containers:

The event was run with one main summit container where all attendees came together and where the whole group generative 'Open Space' session was held. This was run on one event platform developed by the event production company hired to provide the summit's technical support. That was supplemented by five separate Zoom sessions that created a separate space for each executive team to work simultaneously. These separate Zoom sessions also had breakout spaces to subdivide each executive team into small groups if needed.

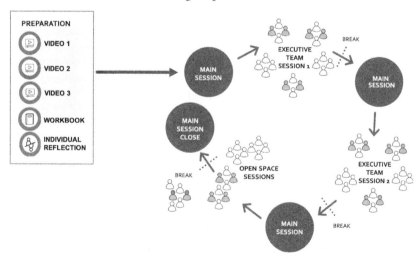

Figure 8: Executive Summit high-level design

Figure 8 above shows the high-level design for the Summit incorporating the preparation and session flow. The session flow shows how the day was split between main sessions—where all teams attended together, and executive team sessions where each team went off to work on their own on a shared topic before re-joining with the whole group in the next main session.

Design for the Day

Main Session 1:
This opening session was run by the Group CEO, Group HRD, and the Summit Host. It set the scene for the day and raised four key questions that would be covered during the day:

- Why is the Leadership Framework important to me and our business?

- What conversations are we going to have about this in our business?

- What does success look like when the leadership framework has been brought to life?

- How will I, and the rest of our executive team, bring this to life?

Executive Team Session 1:
Each of the executive teams joined their own team's virtual meeting, where they were supported by a host and technical host to create their Leadership Framework narrative for success. The teams split into smaller breakout groups as required during this session. At the end of this session, all executive teams returned to the main meeting.

Main Session 2:
On returning to the Main Session, each executive team shared their team's narrative, with some space for reactions, responses, and shared meaning-making. They were then briefed in preparation for the second Executive Team Session.

Executive Team Session 2:
Each team returned to their own virtual meeting space to explore their collective leadership and the leadership roles they felt they excelled at

and were least confident with. They each brought the outputs from their pre-work into this session and agreed on a shared pivotal leadership behavior that would be their first visible endorsement of the leadership framework. The team's split into smaller breakout groups as required during this session.

Main Session 3:
The Open Space topic of 'How could we bring life to the leadership framework?' framed a series of generative conversations in multiple breakout rooms, with scribes supporting the capturing of ideas onto a shared document. At the end of the open space session, the outputs were shared. Individuals identified ideas and initiatives they had the energy to move forward with, and cross-business collaborative teams were formed.

Main Session Close:
Reflections and feedback from all participants were gathered on a live word cloud.

Closing reflections from the Group CEO and Group HRD encouraged commitment and continued momentum from this first collaborative work.

The Summit Hosting Team

With 60+ attendees, the requirements for production support for the summit was beyond any of the prior sessions. A professional conferencing company provided the technical and production support, enabling my colleagues and me to focus on the design and facilitation.

There was an overall Summit Host for the main container (the Group Director of Communications), and a skilled host and a technical host supported each executive team container. My role was as design architect for the Summit, plus hosting one of the executive teams.

The Summit team include the following roles:

- Production Company. This was an experienced events production company with its own virtual event platform. It provided the technical content and project support for the whole event. They ran a 'studio' for presentations in the main session, provided the five Zoom accounts for the Executive Team sessions, technical support, and made everything work.

- Summit Host. Provided the narrative for the summit, connecting each element, provided guidance and briefing for activities.

- Summit Co-host. Monitored and responded to chat comments/questions, and observed/responded to group dynamics.

- Graphic Facilitator. Visually captured the themes from the main sessions.

- Key Speakers. Provided brief presentations from the 'Summit Studio', and took part in their respective executive team session,

- Executive Team Session (Host, Producer, and Scribe) each team session had a host who guided the team through the activity, a producer who provided the technical support for breakout rooms, and a scribe who captured the outputs from the session to be shared with the whole group.

The hosting team was involved in full briefings and technical and content rehearsals in the lead up to the summit.

Change Project Reflections

Stepping back and reflecting on the entire change process, I want to share what emerged that was unexpected and what I would do differently. We achieved our overall aim, which was to co-create a leadership framework that set leadership expectations into the future. Across each of the businesses, there were highly engaged leaders who had contributed to the framework's content and how the new framework emerged and was shaped by a large proportion of the workforce. At the end of the co-creation process, there was visible endorsement and energy to integrate the framework into aspects of leaders' daily lives that needed little encouragement to get started.

Through the lens of the Dialogic OD enablers of emergence, narrative, and generativity, the design encouraged emergence in the way people were brought together in new and novel groupings to explore a shared topic in ways they hadn't before. New narratives were shared through the formal and informal networks within and between businesses. These included stories of people being invited to take part whose voices were not normally heard, opening up to the possibility of a different way of leadership. The entire process generated new ways of working, new relationships, and new possibilities for future collaboration across the group, as well as a new image of leadership that was attractive and stimulated new actions. There had been a collective experience of previously unimagined ways of thinking, creating, and acting together.

What emerged that was unexpected?

There were many unexpected things as I've never previously run a project like this entirely on a virtual platform. The main one is the confirmation that it is possible to run a large co-creation project like this entirely in virtual spaces. I had not heard of anything like it before 2020, and it's easy to overlook just how significant this is in how we do Dialogic OD. Also, it confirmed what we could achieve when our environment changes so quickly and unexpectedly. Some of the topics below were commented on by the client as being unusual in their organization's culture.

1. New and novel narratives: COVID 19 and the Group's response to the pandemic created a huge disturbance in the deeply held patterns of leading and relating. The project's timing meant it emerged as something novel and new amid this disturbance.

    a. It provided something tangible for the businesses to focus on while everything else was uncertain. While some may say adding more novelty during a time of crisis may not be wise, in this case there was sufficient stability in the system due to the action taken on the operational sites to absorb this newness. Plus, there was clear endorsement and sponsorship from the CEO.

    b. This combined with our intention to involve less-heard voices from across the system, our style of offering participation and co-creation, and the way we adopted novel styles of communicating and engaging those who wanted to be involved.

2. Energy and momentum: The program's pace generated energy, momentum, and a ripple through the informal networks as the approach was different from previous approaches. The CEO's launch video created an immediate response from a surprising number of people who had energy and enthusiasm for getting involved. The fact that anyone who stepped forward was involved in some way continued to build the energy and momentum.

3. Engagement: Working virtually made attending a session very easy, no matter where people were located. That enabled us to get wider and more diverse perspectives together than in face-to-face workshops. People from different hierarchical levels and diverse backgrounds felt included and valued, and had conversations they wouldn't have been able to have, nor been invited to. As most other initiatives were halted at the time, only a small handful were continued through the pandemic, which reduced the competing 'noise' in the system for people's time and attention. As a result, engagement levels were high.

4. Being fully present: Contrary to the prevailing culture, people turned up and were fully present at the workshops. They weren't distracted by emails or leaving meetings to take calls; they were engaged, focused, and contributed fully. I believe this was partly due to the novelty factor of virtual working, partly due to the project being run differently from any others they had experienced, and partly due to the reduction in the number of other initiatives taking place and needing their time.

5. Technology novelty and innovation: People weren't used to virtual working and using Zoom. Once they attended a session, they realized how productive working virtually could be. They loved working in breakout rooms and using the whiteboards.

6. Buzz across the network: Developing people internally to host sessions and become Zoom Magicians created a real buzz across the network where people talked about the sessions and their involvement. This encouraged others to step forward, made people curious to learn more and attend sessions they had been invited to, and demonstrated a business commitment to development.

7. Raising visibility and credibility of an internal change team: The project team worked closely with a relatively new internal change team who so far hadn't gained the internal visibility and traction they'd hoped for. They led the organizing of different workshops, planning and scheduling over 600 people's attendance. They tapped into their internal networks to help us reach and engage the more challenging front line leaders, without whom the richness of perspective would have been lost. As a result, the team's profile and

credibility reached new levels, and they have since been involved with more high-profile projects.

8. Speed of adoption: with high levels of engagement and enthusiasm for this work, many teams in each of the businesses have quickly adopted the new framework. They are integrating it into their work in a way that hasn't been present before. In some ways, this was expected as my previous experiences of co-created participatory approaches often generate a high level of energy and action. This was confirmation that these approaches work when applied in a virtual environment

What would I do differently?

1. Make greater use of collaborative platforms. I would spend more time exploring the options for using collaborative platforms with the client and encouraging them to adopt a simple version of asynchronous and real-time working on Mural or another platform to enhance:

- Preparation work before workshops to build relationships and prepare for contribution.

- The way the outputs from the Co-Creation Workshops were captured to allow the real-time outputs to be seen by everyone rather than being individually captured in a separate document. That would also help to:

  - Share outputs more widely for continued contribution, so people could see what had already been captured and build on that. Especially those people not attending the co-creation workshops but still wanting to contribute their ideas to the new framework.

  - Sort and harvest themes from the Co-Creation sessions, speeding up the development of the draft framework.

- Creating a living record of the co-creation process, enabling real-time updates as work progressed. That could be captured on a Mural / Miro board or a centrally held document on an intranet.

- Curating the development history of the new leadership framework so the organization could visibly learn from their first cross-business collaborative project.

2. Lead and shape more stakeholder engagement within each business, incorporating a way to test stakeholder engagement in each business. There were different levels of engagement depending on who had spoken to them. I would offer more support to those doing the stakeholder engagement.

3. More time: the sheer scale of planning and scheduling the program in its virtual format took more time than expected and more time than I had experienced on similar projects in a physical place. Each element of socialization, stakeholder engagement, designing and planning the virtual interventions program needed more attention as we developed and refined new approaches that worked in virtual spaces. Even with more virtual OD consulting experience, and greater familiarization with virtual platforms, it is easy to underestimate how much time needs to be allowed. That will also depend on the levels of technical maturity within the organization.

Future of Virtual Dialogic OD

This concluding chapter looks at how two different aspects of technology are evolving and shifting how we work. I conclude with the thought that, despite the ever-evolving advances in technology, our ongoing success as Dialogic OD practitioners relies more on the choices we make—choices to best sequence and configure the design of virtual spaces, along with our ability to bring the best of our presence and skills in human systems in service of the client systems we work in and support.

Disruption

Could any of us have imagined the massive changes to how we now go about our work as Dialogic OD consultants? I certainly couldn't have predicted what was in store. As I reflect back, I appreciate the pioneering spirit and willingness to experiment that has emerged in me since March 2020.

With that in mind, there's a part of me that doesn't think I can do justice to look into Dialogic OD's future in virtual spaces. The continued explosion of new technologies and new ways of using existing technology in a business environment are happening even as I type this. What was 'new' is suddenly 'everyday' or 'old hat', and I wonder how much of this will still be 'future' by the time you are reading this chapter.

However, there are some things that I am confident will continue to support the evolution of our paradigm shift into virtual OD:

- A constant explosion of technological advances.

- Businesses and organizations reimagining the workplace and reviewing the need for physical office space.

- The need for clear principles and thoughtful design to support clients' resolving tricky challenges and emerging unknowns.

- The need for skillful consultants who can create and host spaces where people come together to explore, generate, make meaning, and act.

- The need for consultants who can use technology to create spaces that enable collaborative and participative working, who recognize the importance of relational and dialogic based work, and can flex their presence and impact in a virtual space.

Here are some of the developments emerging on current platforms and advancements in virtual reality that are part of our future.

Embracing and incorporating developments on current platforms

The development and enhancement of current virtual meeting platforms continue to shift the possibilities for consulting in virtual spaces. Zoom and MS Teams regularly release new features and are starting to integrate more flexibility into their offering with add on apps. At the time of writing, Zaaps (Zoom Apps) are available that integrate external applications with the Zoom platform, and MS Teams introduced breakout rooms in December 2020.

There are things as a Dialogic OD consultant that I'd like to see added to the offer on the virtual meeting platforms:

- Interactivity options available in the 'waiting room' where people can connect while waiting to join.

- Spaces where spontaneous conversations and serendipitous connections can happen.

- The ability to 'listen in' to a conversation in a breakout room without having to join it, so that you only join the room if support or guidance is needed and don't disrupt the group at work

Collaborative platforms

The options for digital collaborative platforms is growing, with new offerings coming onto the market. Some of these integrate what were separate platforms into one easy to access space. *Howspace* describes itself as an artificial intelligence-powered digital collaboration and dialogue-driven facilitation platform that can be used for organizational transformation. *Session Lab* is a platform to help create, share and organize workshop content with a library of pre-designed workshop sessions on various topics.

Whether we choose to embrace some of these newer integrated platforms or continue to work with those we are familiar with, there are undoubtedly opportunities to enhance the experiences of working virtually. We can enhance design by co-creating programs or workshop designs on collaborative platforms with colleagues and clients. These can be asynchronous, synchronous or both. This provides ways to widen the frame of participation, work with more geographically-dispersed teams, and generate a single record of iterative and emergent working accessible to all.

Virtual reality meets Dialogic OD

Virtual reality platforms (2-D and 3-D) are starting to emerge in the world of social gatherings, networking, and business events.

2-D virtual reality platforms:

Many of these two-dimensional platforms are changing how people come together outside the main meeting platforms. They are opening up new possibilities to create formal and informal conversation and dialogue spaces. They create movement and choice for participants that isn't present in Zoom, Microsoft Teams or Google Meet. Here are three that I have experienced:

1. **High Fidelity:** A social virtual reality platform.

2. **Wonder:** A virtual space where people can meet and talk.

3. **Remo:** A virtual networking and conference platform with virtual office space.

High Fidelity is an audio-only experiences with virtual backgrounds viewed on your computer. *Wonder* is an audio and video experience. On both you can create any background setting you want, hosting a meeting or social gathering on a beach, in a castle, or wherever you choose.

Remo uses live video and chat to connect people in meeting or conference rooms or office settings. You can create your own conference room layout for the configuration you want. They all work on standard screens and don't incorporate VR headsets.

How they work:

When you join these platforms, an 'avatar' shape represents you on the screen. You can upload a photo or use another image to identify yourself. In *Remo*, your avatar is supplemented by a live video that starts when you are talking to others in a private conversation.

The audio experience is generated as you move around the 'set' or 'room' and you have conversations with another person or with groups of people. The closer you move towards an individual or group, or when you enter a room, you start to hear their conversation and can join in when you are close enough. As you move away or exit a room, their voices fade out as they would in real life. Movement is generated either through your mouse clicks or with the directional keys on your keyboard.

On *High Fidelity*, you can create whatever 'background set' you want, from an informal social gathering in someone's house to a more formal business environment with separate conversation circles set up. These background sets can have landmark objects and meeting spaces, videos, music, and other links for people to follow and access on demand.

On *Wonder*, you can create the visual imagery and conversation spaces in the way you want them, thus guiding people into spaces for topics of mutual interest. You can broadcast videos or speak to everyone to prompt and guide discussions.

Remo creates a top-down view of a map which shows either a conference layout of small tables and a stage, or an office layout. In the *Remo* conference, people can move freely from table to table to have different conversations, listen to main stage presentations, and move off into breakout rooms. At a large event, there are multiple floors that people can freely move between, with total choice as to where they sit.

Used alongside formal sessions, these platforms open up some of the things that are currently missing from the meeting platforms:

- The ability for people to move around and spontaneously gather in small groups.

- Dialogic methodologies like Open Space, World Café,

Appreciative Inquiry could be effectively run on these platforms.

- You can choose to sit and work in a circle.

- You can complete a shared task, play games, discuss a topic or just chat.

- You can recapture some of the informal and spontaneous conversations that happen in the 'in-between spaces' and coffee breaks.

- Participants have much more ownership over where they go and who they talk to.

3-D virtual reality platforms—online gaming meets OD?

New three-dimensional (3-D) platforms integrate online gaming approaches into collaboration, virtual working, and education, improving the sense of live interaction experienced by participants. The online gaming world is enormous; incorporating virtual, augmented and mixed reality. It is how many current and next-generation leaders spend their leisure time.

VirBELA is a 3D immersive collaboration platform that uses a game engine to create spaces for collaborative teamwork, business learning, virtual workshops, and conference events.

Conference and team suites are available that have a number of large and small group environments. Personalized avatars that you create yourself allow you to walk, run, and teleport around a venue. There's even an option for your avatar to dance!

Once in your conference suite, you can listen to presentations, watch videos, have planned or spontaneous conversations, chat on text, and exchange virtual business cards. Private conversation zones can be set up in zoned areas. These can be locked if secure conversations are needed. There are informal networking spaces that replicate coffee areas and enable spontaneous conversations where you hear a conversation more clearly as you move towards the people talking to each other.

These social-based virtual reality platforms are exciting places for us to experiment, play, and continue to move our work into new virtual spaces. They can be used to overcome some of the lost experiences that meeting platforms don't give us—particularly, interactions where informal and spontaneous conversations happen and where we feel a sense of freedom to move into spaces we choose to go.

Holographic portals

Beyond the world of 3D virtual reality is the holographic portal. This leading-edge technology has been developed where a real-time full-body hologram can enable someone to be beamed into a hologram box in your room or office. As this technology advances, there could be a point when CEOs could beam holograms of themselves into multiple office locations around the world and conduct a meeting or engage in conversation with their customers or stakeholders.

Final thoughts

Technology is an enabler, but it can also be a distraction. There was an element of technology anxiety in conversations with colleagues at the start of the pandemic; anxiety that led to concerned questions like, 'Am I using the best platform?' and 'Is there something that I need to know that I don't?'

Earlier in 2020, there was undoubtedly a 'first adopter' advantage, with those consultants more familiar with how to get the best from the technology appearing more confident and skillful. Now there seems to be a levelling of the playing field as people are catching up and building their skills and confidence.

There is a danger that we get dazzled by the latest technology and that it gets in the way of preventing us from doing great work in virtual spaces. We need to know enough and be confident in using it, to be able to meet our clients where they are at, not to dazzle them with our technological brilliance or lack of it. Too much technology can become a barrier for attendees as they focus more on the need/desire to 'get it right' than on the contributions we want them to make.

Discernment

- As Dialogic OD practitioners, we need to be discerning and use what we know thoughtfully, using technology as an enabler for our work to shape and host virtual spaces where generative dialogue and co-creation are in the foreground.

- Don't over-engineer the technology. Hone your craft, and continue developing your use of self to create transformative moments.

- There is even more of a need for great design and great hosting. As new technology's distraction fades, the importance of relational work, human connection, co-creation and dialogue-based work grows.
- Embrace more asynchronous working combined with synchronous working live. The blend needed will be shaped by the program arc and meeting the client culture where it is at.
- Consider when a blend of place and space is required. What aspects of our work need to be done in a physical place when it becomes more accessible again?

The way I interact, engage and collaborate with others in a virtual space has changed so much of the way I work. I now can't imagine what it was like before, nor can I imagine only working in the physical place again. That is the true meaning of transformation—not going back to how things used to be after a fundamental change in beliefs and how I see the world.

A paradigm shift?

There has been a revolution in how we work, and I believe there will continue to be an evolution of the field of virtual dialogic OD.

Looking forward, as a field of practitioners, we are facing a paradigm shift of our own in response to how businesses and organizations are reimagining the future of work. We are presented with an amazing opportunity to reimagine the value that Dialogic OD approaches can offer business and the global communities in which we live. Technology and working in virtual spaces allow us to work globally in a way we've not been able to do before.

To do this, we need to be willing to challenge ourselves and how we present ourselves to current and future clients and stay at the edge of our practice as skilful designers, hosts and intervenors. We need to lean into spaces that might bring us discomfort and uncertainty as we experience things we've not previously seen in ourselves, in others, in business, in technology, and in society. These can provide rich opportunities for learning, human development and growth.

References

Brown, B. (2010). *The power of vulnerability.* TEDxHouston. https://www.ted.com/talks/brene_brown_the_power_of_vulnerability

Bushe, G.R. (2020). *The dynamics of generative change.* BMI Publishing.

Bushe, G.R. (2010). *Being the container in dialogic OD. Practicing Social Change,* 1:2, 10-15.

Bushe, G.R. and Marshak, R.J. (2015). (Eds.). *Dialogic organization development: The theory and practice of transformational change.* Berrett-Kohler.

Cambridge Online Dictionary, Cambridge University Press (2020). https://dictionary.cambridge.org/dictionary/english/intervention

Cheung-Judge, M-Y and Holbeche, L. (2015). *Organization development: A practitioner's guide for OD and HR.* Kogan-Page.

Chidiac, M-A. (2018). *Relational Organisational Gestalt.* Routledge.

Csikszentmihalyi, M (2008). *Flow: The psychology of optimal experience.* Harper.

Delizonna, L. (2017). High-performing teams need psychological safety. Here's how to create it. *Harvard Business Review Digital Archives,* available at https://store.hbr.org/product/high-performing-teams-need-psychological-safety-here-s-how-to-create-it/h03tk7?sku=H03TK7-PDF-ENG.

Denham-Vaughan, S. (2010). *The liminal space and twelve action practices for gracious living.* British Gestalt Journal. 19(2): 34-45.

Corrigan, C. (2007, November 20). Facilitating AND Hosting, *http://www.chriscorrigan.com/parkinglot/facilitating-vs-hosting/*

Edmondson, A.C. (2018). *The fearless organization.* Wiley

Halifax, J. (2010). *Compassion and the true meaning of empathy.* TEDWomen 2010. https://www.ted.com/talks/joan_halifax_compassion_and_the_true_meaning_of_empathy?language=en

Hanna, T. (1988). *Somatics: Reawakening the mind's control of movement, flexibility and health.* Addison-Wesley.

Gillespie, C. (2020). *Zoom Fatigue: Why video chat is exhausting you right now, and what to do about it.* Health. https://www.health.com/condition/infectious-diseases/coronavirus/zoom-fatigue

Jamieson, D.W. & Davidson, J.E. (2019). Advancing thinking and practice on use of self. *Organization Development Journal*, 37:1, 39-53.

Kahn, W.A. (1990). Psychological conditions of personal engagement and disengagement at work. *Academy of Management Journal, 33*, 4: 692-724.

Leema, A. (2017). *The Digital age on the couch.* Routledge

Lewis, S. (2020). *Co-creating planning teams for dialogic OD: From entry to event.* BMI Publishing.

Marshak, R.J. (2020). *Dialogic process consulting: Generative meaning-making in action.* BMI Publishing.

McKergow, M. (2020). *Hosting generative change: Creating containers for creativity and commitment.* BMI Publishing.

Nevis, E.C. (1997). *Organizational consulting: A gestalt approach.* The Gestalt Institute of Cleveland Press.

Rainey Tolbert, M.A. and Hanafin, J. (2006). *Use of self in OD Consulting: What matters is presence.* In Jones B and Brazzel, M (Eds), *The NTL Handbook of Organization Development and Change* (pp. 69-82). Pfeiffer.

Reddy, W.B. (1994). *Intervention skills: Process consultation for small groups and teams.* Pfieffer.

Scarrott, J. (2020). Personal communication, September 1, 2020.

Schein, E.H. (1969). *Process consultation: Its role in organization development.* Reading, MA: Addison-Wesley Publishers.

Shaw, P. (2002). *Changing conversations in organizations.* Routledge.

Tschudy, T. (2006). *An OD Map: The essence of organization development.* In Jones B and Brazzel, M (Eds), *The NTL Handbook of Organization Development and Change* (pp. 157-176). Pfeiffer.

BMI Series in Dialogic OD

The BMI series in Dialogic OD, inspired by the original Addison-Wesley Series in OD, is a series of short, 100 page volumes written by experienced Dialogic OD practitioners. Edited by Gervase Bushe and Bob Marshak, each narrowly focuses on one specific aspect of Dialogic OD practice and provides consultants with tested, practical models and processes, along with case examples to make the models come alive.

Dialogic Process Consulting: Generative Meaning-Making in Action

https://b-m-institute.com/books/dialogic-process-consulting/

Robert Marshak introduces a subtle but powerful dialogic OD method that coaches and consultants can use to help clients address limiting assumptions and create new possibilities. The phrase "generative meaning-making in action" captures the essence of the approach. You will learn how to identify and address out-of-awareness mindsets during everyday conversations, how to deeply listen for the implicit mindsets that influence meaning-making in individuals, groups and organizations, and how to intervene through transforming talk to challenge or change them.

The Dynamics of Generative Change

https://b-m-institute.com/books/the-dynamics-of-generative-change/

Gervase Bushe steps you through the Generative Change Model, a way to approach organizational change more aligned with today's needs for an agile and engaged workforce than planned change methods. We follow the case of Consolidated Construction Materials Supply, 200 poorly engaged employees inside a large, traditional construction company. Organized into three fragmented units, this low-tech warehouse and distribution operation transformed into a highly engaged, collaborative, agile and fully digitized one in a little more than two years after the first phone call between the consultant and the Director. They accomplished this without a vision, without a plan, without training, any resistance to change, and only 1 external OD consultant. The book provides advice on the key issues in leading an emergent, generative change process.

Hosting Generative Change: Creating Containers for Creativity and Commitment

http://b-m-institute.com/books/hosting-generative-change/

When the future is uncertain and the past is contested, good hosting can bring hope and co-operation into the present. Any Dialogic OD practice will bring people together for creative conversations, expanded horizons, mutual connection and committed action. The way these events are hosted can make all the difference. **Mark McKergow** brings over a decade of research into the etiquette of hosting in different cultures and eras and combines it with three decades of practice in organizational development and change. The book offers an image of superb hosting as a mix of detailed planning and openness to whatever emerges, taking the lead when needed, with the intent of stepping back as quickly as possible so participants can lead themselves. The book offers a framework of six hosting roles to help navigate the inevitable ups and downs of working with large (and small) groups.

The Team Discovered: Dialogic Team Coaching

http://b-m-institute.com/books/the-team-discovered/

This hopeful, poignant, and deeply insightful book brings the wisdom of Dialogic OD and the heritage of Diagnostic OD into an expansive view of how to best support teams in a world of immense diversity and attention poverty. **Bennett Bratt** offers a new approach to team development that meets today's teams where they live: in a complex world with intense demands and precious little time. This book challenges widely used approaches to team development that utilize data showing a gap between current and desirable team performance. Most methods presume some kind of evaluative comparison is helpful: comparison to other groups, comparison to large data sets, comparison to best practices, comparison to a theoretical ideal. Instead, Ben explains why a dialogic approach to the use of questionnaire data is better at helping teams author their own narrative of effectiveness, one they will own and live into. While showing how to make data useful, Bratt persuasively argues that comparison is at best, a distraction and at worst, debilitating. The book illustrates how to bring the mindsets and tools of Dialogic OD to team coaching through an extended case example.

Future Planned Volumes

Co-creating Planning Teams for Dialogic OD: From Entry to Event

Sarah Lewis

Entry and Contracting for Dialogic OD

Tova Averbuch

It's a Thing: Using Transactional Objects in Dialogic OD

Tonnie van der Zouwen

If you have an idea for a short (under 30,000 words) book on a specific aspect of Dialogic OD practice, please contact either Gervase (**bushe@sfu.ca**) or Bob (**bobmarshak@aol.com**) to discuss.

Printed in Great Britain
by Amazon